REPEAT BUSINESS

by

Larry W. Dennis

Rising Tide Publishing
Portland, Oregon

Other books by Larry W. Dennis
Empowering Leadership
How To Turbo Charge You

First Printing 1992
Second Printing 1993
Third Printing 1994

Repeat Business

Dedication

To our eldest son, Larry Dennis, Jr., who, at age 21, sold more than $250,000 worth of ladies' shoes in one year. Without Larry's encouragement, support, and companionship over the last several years, I would never have completed this book.

Thank you, son.

Introduction

You are reading a WOW of a book. As you read, master and apply the timeless principles that Larry Dennis writes about, you will wow yourself with the amount of business that you create and repeatedly re-serve. Best of all, you will feel good while you are doing well.

Larry W. Dennis is an extraordinary speaker, thinker, trainer, writer, businessman and salesman. I am proud to call him my friend of fifteen years. He has helped thousands of people develop more freedom in their lives, more money and improved lifestyles.

Drink deeply of the wisdom in this book. I recommend you read this with five different colored highlighter pens. In super learning, we have discovered that as you highlight in different colors, you perturb different brain cells and stimulate greater content retention. Additionally, I encourage you to write notes in the margins of what you think and feel about what you read. I have read every word. I love it. My copy is brightly colored with multiple highlights on every page.

There are three tests of great communication:
1) How long the thoughts you read live in
   your memory.
2) How much they serve you.
3) How much you re-communicate them.

Larry's book so influenced me while I was traveling to a seminar in Las Vegas, that I told an audience of two thousand doctors two of the stories with full acknowledgement to him. Larry's thinking is vitally alive in my mind; it serves me greatly, and I recommended it to the doctors who heard me praise Larry Dennis.

Likewise, I respectfully encourage you to read Larry's book. Think about it. Apply it to your business, practice, your trade and family. Share these vibrant, delightfully delicious thought-bites of information with those you love, your clients, customers, patients and patrons, your suppliers, your staff and your friends.

Let us take the ideas in *Repeat Business* and put them to work to get our economy booming and zooming forward. Together, doing this, we can go to new heights of service, success, prosperity and wealth.

Larry has written the manifesto to obtain repeat business. I recommend that you read and re-read this book until you own the ideas. Attend one of Larry's seminars with your team. If you will do that and apply these *Repeat Business* principles, you will be building an empire worthy of the greatness within you.

Congratulations in advance.

Dr. Mark Victor Hansen
Newport Beach, California

Repeat Business

Table of Contents

Chapter 1

The best way to increase your value to your employer is to help increase repeat business. Repeat business comes from loyal customers who can't be wooed away by the over-zealous claims of competitors. Predictable customers form the foundation of a successful business. Repeat customers cost us little in promotion and advertising costs. Repeat customers are the key to continuing profitability. **Who signs your paycheck?** The customer signs your paycheck. Every business is dependent on customers. Yet staggering numbers of businesses fail every day mostly because they do not have enough customers! Here are some important reasons for creating enthusiastic repeat customer satisfaction:

1. The customer is the **only** reason for your business in the first place. Every product and service is designed with the customer in mind.

2. It is the customer who **determines** whether your business will prosper and grow. You may have dreams and plans for the future, but it is the customer who will determine whether those dreams come true.

3. The customer **tells** a business which products and services it can sell. People seldom buy things for which they have no need. The successful business must be keenly aware of customer needs.

4. The customer signs your check, **pays**, the rent, utilities and every bill your business receives. Money is the

lifeblood of every business and customers provide an infusion every time they buy

5. A satisfied customer is the **most effective** and **least expensive** form of advertising for any business. How many times have you purchased a product or service from a particular company because someone gave you an enthusiastic recommendation?

No matter what business you are in—retail, professional (doctor, lawyer, accountant), wholesale, restaurant, contractor, plumber—the best way to increase profits is to increase **repeat business**. Gary Bargatze, vice president of Tech Assistance Research in Washington D.C., says it costs far more (up to six times more) to attract one new customer than to keep an old one. By keeping our customers happy, we are more likely to increase market share and profitability. A satisfied customer may tell three people about his good experience while an unsatisfied customer is likely to tell eleven people about his bad experience. And often he exaggerates the tale. It doesn't seem fair, does it? Yet if you look at your own behavior you may find that you are more emotional, more verbal, and more likely to talk about your unhappy experiences than you are your happy, satisfying experiences.

Keep Them Smiling

Dissatisfied customers really hurt our business. Sometimes called the "silent killers," they don't tell you they are unhappy. If they told you, you would do your best to make them happy and correct the situation. Instead, they just go away, tell their friends, and never come back. How many of us have had an experience like the one following and vowed we would never return to that company?

I pulled into a tire store last winter. This store probably spends $2,000 per month on the traditional forms of advertising: display, radio, television, etc. I had needed tires, very expensive tires, on my Porsche 911 SC for several months. It was a cold day. I was greeted by a dirty, scowling, unhappy, sock hat-clad grease monkey who said in a clipped, curt tone, "Can I do something for you? We're closed." This is not the way to secure repeat business or even first time business. I got back in my car and drove away.

Here is a guarantee: each customer who does business with you will have something negative to say about his experience, or something positive, or nothing to say at all. Two of those outcomes are bad! To create a positive story, to be outstanding, our service must exceed customer expectations. We must look for opportunities to give each customer more than he expects or would get when doing business with competitors.

No one can afford unsatisfied customers. Treat your customers as if they are gold—treasure and hoard them. If your service slips below expectations, if your customers feel taken for granted, if you're slipshod in any way, they will find somewhere else to buy apples, bats, cars, dishes, envelopes, fish, gum, and haircuts. Your customers will find someone else to write their will, heal their cough, do their taxes. They will call someone else to fix the Ford, mend the faucet, and file the folders.

When the Small Business Administration asked salespeople why they felt customers stopped buying in their stores most said prices were too high. But when the agency surveyed customers to find out the real reason they changed stores, this is what they found:

2%   died.
3%   moved away.

9%	cited prices.
14%	were dissatisfied with the product.
68%	were treated **indifferently** by salespeople.

Is it easy to please customers? No, it's tougher than ever. John Naisbitt, author of *Megatrends*, calls today "The era of accountability." Customers today are better educated, more price-conscious, and generally expect more service, courtesy, and professionalism for their money than ever before.

Beyond Satisfaction

If we are going to secure repeat business based on service we must eliminate the word "satisfy" from our vocabulary. Often people tell us their job is to satisfy customers and give them what they expect. Satisfying customers sounds too much like meeting expectations, which does little to improve a service reputation. If service is to be our competitive edge, setting bolder goals is a must. Consider:

• Wowing the customer.
• Delighting every customer.
• Making customer interactions memorable.
• Ensuring that customers will "brag" about the service you provide.

It was reported recently in the *New York Times* that the relatively new electronic databases grocers are using have proven, to the surprise and embarrassment of many, that even grocery stores lose 40% of their customers every year.

An article entitled "Speaking the Customers' Language", in United Airlines' magazine *Vis a Vis,* stated that service is the biggest single issue among customers and in the media today. The article tells the story of an

American executive and a prominent businessman from the Far East who were having lunch. The American asked, "What is the most important language for world trade?" expecting the reply to be, "English." The Asian answered, "The most important language for world trade is my customer's language."

Recently the *Harvard Business Review*, under editor Theodore Levit, decided to change its direction. To make more money, a decision was made to change the format of the publication, sell less advertising, and increase subscription and advertising fees. Shorter stories were planned, crisper graphics, and more cartoons. People said it wouldn't work; they predicted a loss of loyal customers and revenue. Initially, the detractors were right, but in a few months the bottom line showed increased profits. Once a customer is a **satisfied, loyal** customer he will pay more money for more services at higher prices.

What can you do to secure and maintain repeat business? That's what this book is about. *Repeat Business* is a practical approach to daily customer satisfaction. You will learn:

- **How to greet customers.**
- **How to handle complaints.**
- **What to do when the customer is kept waiting.**
- **How to handle unexpected questions.**
- **How to remember customers' names.**
- **The importance of follow-through.**
- **And much more.**

Repeat Business will tell you what to say in the variety of situations you encounter every day. You will see how to demonstrate your **R**eliability, understand the personal value gained by going the **E**xtra Mile, be shown simple ways to project a **P**leasant Personality and gain a deeper understanding of the real power of **E**nthusiasm. You will learn the value of going into **A**ction, and be reminded of the positive power of saying **T**hank You. You will find your own way of applying these new insights and you will learn to adapt them to your own situations. If you follow the suggestions in this book, you will remarkably improve the number of repeat customers in your business, have more fun, and your work will take on a renewed sense of adventure and purpose. Following is a test on how your own customer relations stand up. Grade yourself on your results. You may bre surprised on how you come out. Your standing should tell you about how you rank in customer satisfaction.

Customer Relations Test

up:
Here is a test of how your customer relations measure

Do you: **Yes No**
1. Greet customers by name when possible?   ___ ___
2. Make every customer feel special and
important?   ___ ___
3. Handle customer complaints quickly,
courteously and to the customers' satisfaction?   ___ ___
4. Know how and where to re-direct customers'
questions if you can't help them?   ___ ___
5. Say "Thank You" in special ways to every
customer?   ___ ___
6. Project a confident and professional image
that builds customer trust?   ___ ___
7. Know how to efficiently handle several
customers at once?   ___ ___
8. Take time to listen to what the customer

is saying?   — —

9. Do some little extra thing for every
customer?   — —

10. Know how to tell a customer "no" when
necessary?   — —

11. Recognize and solve customers'
problems before they become critical?   — —

12. Add value to every transaction with the
joy of your enthusiasm?   — —

Total Number of "Yeses" ___

If you answered **Yes** to <u>all of the above</u>, congratulations! You rate "excellent" in customer contact, service and satisfaction.

If you answered **Yes** to <u>7 to 9</u>, you are doing a good job, and there's room for improvement. In this book, you will learn the insights and techniques that'll give you the "winning edge" your customers will notice and appreciate, insuring repeat business and greater job satisfaction.

If you answered **Yes** to <u>6 or less</u>, "Repeat Business—the Key to Profit," could Turbo-Charge your performance...with amazing results to yours and your company's bottom line.

Now **you have to decide how good you want to be.**

• Do you want to be no better or worse than anyone else?

• Do you want to be "among the best"?

• Do you want to be the best in your company?

• Do you want to be distinctively better than anyone else?

Circle the statement that best describes your "goal."

Chapter 2

— R —

Reliability

"Never promise more than you can perform."

— *Publilius Syrus*

The first of six principles in acquiring and maintaining repeat business is demonstrating **reliability.** Webster defines reliability as "that [which] can be relied on."

Our definition:

- Doing what you <u>say</u> you are going to do.
- Doing what you <u>imply</u> you are going to do
- Doing what <u>needs</u> to be done.
- <u>Keeping</u> your word.

We all know people who over promise and under-deliver. They will promise almost anything, but you can't count on them. The rule for proving reliability is **under-promise and over-deliver.**

What do customers want in customer service? In *Training: the Magazine of Human Resources Development*

(August 1988), the Forum Corporation reported that "customer service excellence" means different things to companies and their customers. The quality of a customer's experience with a company depends on the organization's *reliability*, its assurance that employees will be knowledgeable and courteous, the appearance of the facilities and the personnel, the degree of caring shown to customers, and willingness of staff to be helpful and to provide prompt service. Customers rated reliability as the most important aspect of customer service and physical appearances as the least important, but companies that try to improve customer service usually begin by concentrating on physical appearances. *Forum Corporation* suggested that companies would be better served by training employees to be more reliable and responsive. One strong instance of lack of reliability will prejudice a person against a service provider for a long time. My own case is an example:

On a Friday morning I left my house at about 6:00 a.m. heading for the Portland Airport to catch a 7:09 a.m. flight to make a 9:00 a.m. appointment in Seattle. The day before I left my wife had insisted I fly to save the wear and tear of driving, even though the trip by highway is only three hours.

So away I went. I got on the plane, met a couple of graduates of my training classes, and we passed time visiting while the plane was readying for departure. Finally, at about 7:50 we were told that an antenna on the plane had been damaged by the ground crew. A part had been located, but there would be considerable further delay. They recommended that all Seattle bound passengers deplane, and go to Horizon Air. I power walked to get from Gate D to Gate A. Only to discover there were no seats available for the 8:00 flight. I was promised a seat on the 8:30. You guessed it; when I got to the stairway of the plane, I was told "Sorry, no more room on this one." I called Seattle and rescheduled my trip.

I have driven to Seattle on my last six trips!

Promptness

Promptness is the first sign of reliability.

If you agree to meet a customer at 12:00 o'clock for lunch and get there at 12:15, what does your customer think? If you are supposed to start work at 8 a.m., be there at 7:45 a.m. If you have an appointment for noon, be there at 11:50 a.m. Why? Because companies know they can rely on employees who are on time. Customers know they can count on companies who deliver as promised, and patients have better relationships with doctors who don't keep them waiting.

Recently a doctor made me wait over thirty minutes for our scheduled appointment. On my second visit, it happened again. I have found another doctor who keeps his appointments as agreed. My time is valuable. I have better things to do than sit in a *waiting* room. Doctors have done such a great job of keeping us waiting that we have even dubbed the reception area "The Waiting Room"!

The American consumer's number one complaint is being kept waiting. Suppliers who make dealers wait lose dealers; stores who keep customers waiting lose customers. Doctors who make patients wait lose patients. This lack of responsiveness may have given rise to the popularity of the walk-in clinic. Walk-in clinics are less than ten years old; it is estimated that over 36% of Americans use them. Taking this one step further is the doctor who makes house calls from her fully equipped medical van.

So prove your reliability by being punctual.

In Stock

I shop regularly at a store that advertises: "You'll find it at Harry's." This is an extraordinarily important promise. It is a great advertising slogan for a great store with a wide selection. When they are out of what they've advertised, I am upset, let down, taken advantage of, and I feel I can't rely on them. Lack of stock probably indicates poor buying practices or a poor reordering system. For example, I wanted a four-inch adjustable clamp to use on a dryer vent: Out of Stock! Not just in one of their stores, but in four of the locations I visited. I later found a clamp "in stock", in the right size, at a competitors store.

From the same store I needed a light bulb for my bug zapper; Out of Stock! The manager told me that no store in town would have one. I found the bulb in the store of a national competitor. I needed base insulation for my garage door; Out of stock in two stores, in stock in the third store, but too short! A part of being reliable is being "in stock" and staying that way. Regardless of your position, make it your responsibility to be in stock in your area of your business.

Rainchecks for customers on out-of-stock products cost more than money in administrative costs. They cost us image, confidence and repeat business. When a raincheck is necessary, get the customer's name and phone number. Call the customer when the merchandise comes in and say: "Ms. Customer, we have your __(order item)__ in stock now. I am holding one for you. I have your name on it in layaway. Will it be convenient for you to stop by in the next few days? Please say hello when you stop by to pick it up. I will work hard and make every effort to keep stock on hand. Thank you for your patience with us."

Pricing

If you advertise competitive prices—implicitly or implied—don't let your customers find the same merchandise at a significantly better price somewhere else. Your customer may feel taken advantage of, abused. Your customer may feel you lied. Your otherwise loyal customer may start to look around, check prices, and switch to another supplier. **Trust, not trickery, will keep customers loyal.**

A good example of how a customer thinks about pricing was demonstrated when my wife found a private branded talcum powder packaged the same as a national brand, at thirty percent less. She made the discovery at a national mass merchandise store. We naturally concluded that it was the same powder we always bought from our preferred local store. We also concluded that all other merchandise might be less expensive at the national store. The issue was not the ninety cents difference in price; it was the customer's perception of being treated unfairly. The result was loss of loyalty and repeat business.

Businesses lose opportunities to engage customers, as a result of poorly trained employees and managers. A shopping trip demonstrated for me the lack of interest in a customer's remarks.

I made ten trips to nine different stores before I found the part I needed for a plumbing job on our old house. This gave me an unusual opportunity to compare pricing and inventory of nine similar stores. At one of the stores I asked the department manager why his prices were so high. He shrugged his shoulders and said, "We're usually pretty competitive." I felt like saying, "Oh, really - prove it." I wanted him to enthusiastically tell me prices were high because quality was better. Or to ask my name, get my number, tell me he would pass on my comment to his buyer and get back to me. Suffice it to say, his response didn't show an attitude of wanting more information on how to insure repeat business.

Welcome

I went to the lumberyard late one afternoon to buy some caulk and ready-mix. I arrived shortly before five o'clock. The sign outside the door said "Open" but the company trucks were lined up as if the store was closed. I thought to myself, "If this door is locked, I'm going to be very upset." As I think back on the experience, I was ready for a fight. Well, the door was open so I went inside. The focus of attention in the store was, "Let's close, now." I could feel it. All the salespeople were focused on closing. They were counting out the till, summarizing the day's business, and were eager to leave.

Finally someone said, in a rather flat way, "May I help you?" We talked briefly about what I wanted. Just as I was leaving the store it turned five o'clock, the time the store was officially supposed to close. The minute the clock turned to five they turned the bolt on the door. They had to unlock the door to let me out. I guess I'm one of those troublesome, "last-minute" customers. And I thought **all** customers were supposed to be valued and treated courteously.

If you want to assure that your customers will keep coming back be ready for them before the doors open and after the final sale of the day.

Special Requests

If you tell a customer you will call to find an answer on a needed item, keep your word. Make the call and get back to your customer in a timely manner. If you promise to special order something, follow through. Most of our problems with reliability fall outside of the day to day routines of our business and require extra effort, extra planning. We must have a plan to respond and follow through on special requests. When you're in the press of business, demands are placed on you from every side, internally and externally every minute. You have deadlines to meet, phones to answer, and people to deal with. Following through on promises may require advanced planning.

One way not to forget is to keep a pad of paper handy, entitled "Promises and Follow-Up."

When you get a break, instead of doing the routine, easy tasks, or talking with associates, look at your "Promises" reminder. Follow through, keep your promises, and prove your reliability. You are always better off and further ahead saying "I'm sorry, I can't help you," than to make promises you fail to keep.

"Constant preoccupation with customer service," said Robert E. Levinson, "results in stronger sales and profits. An obsession with providing strong customer service can change ordinary organizations and sales staff into remarkable producers. Subordinates who are indifferent to customer needs, are negligent, or do not show utmost courtesy should be removed. Sales personnel should recognize that service is a team effort, one which should be characterized by strong follow-through and follow-up on previous client contact.

Excuses

Excuses never look good on anyone and customers really don't want to hear half-baked explanations or why they've been disappointed. They want results. Your customers who have been waiting for a product or a service don't really want to know that someone didn't show up because he was sick or that a supplier sent the wrong item, or there was a death in the family of one of the team. Keep your troubles to yourself. "I've got a cold, I think it's the flu; I hurt my back." **Keep your complaints to yourself.** You do not endear yourself to your customer with these wimpy words.

British Airways gave a good example of reliability under pressure. The airline flies the Concorde between New York and London. Recently it found that its plane, the only one of its kind in New York, didn't pass the standards for the flight. What did British Airways do? It gave a complete refund to its passengers, chartered a plane, and flew all the passengers to London—**at no charge!** What are you doing, making excuses or proving your reliability?

Performance Will ContinueTo Outsell Promises

I have tried to contact the people who installed the roof, gutters, and downspouts on my house. I called once a day for over two weeks. They did not return my calls. They will receive no recommendations, no **repeat business** from me. I may end up telling eleven people about my dissatisfaction. What makes things worse is that the company is a member of a national franchise. I am inclined to include **all** of the other tradesmen members of the franchise in my judgement that they cannot be relied on.

Strive to be perceived as reliable and remember:

- **Promptness**; it will impress you client with your eagerness to do business.
- **Keep stock current**; rainchecks cost more than immediate lost sales and money in administrative costs. They tarnish your image and color you as unreliable.
- **Pricing**; keep prices consistent with advertised, implied, implicit promises.
- **Special requests**; keep your promises and go one step further: under promise and over deliver. (See Chapter 2 for more details.)
- **Excuses**; never blame others for your inability to serve your customers
- **Return phone calls**; it only takes a moment and it can make the difference in the customer's perception of your reliability.

Reliability and responsibility are qualities with a similar root. Responsibility means the ability to respond, to take the action needed to do what needs to be done and to be the kind of person everyone can rely on to do the right thing. What a great reputation to have with friends, bosses, competitors and customers alike. It is better to under promise and over deliver. **Reputation is made by many positive acts, and can be lost by one act of neglect (negligence).**

The most important benefit you gain by proving your reliability is your reputation with yourself—your self esteem, belief in yourself, your self confidence. The development of these qualities help to guarantee your long term success.

Return Phone Calls

Return your phone calls and return them promptly. One of the biggest complaints our staff has is the discourteous, inconsiderate person who fails to return phone calls. Often we are involved in selling our services, but it only takes a second to return a call. I have found that the bigger the person I call, the higher up the ladder, the faster he returns my call. I had the occasion recently to call Jim Nordstrom, the president of the Nordstrom Corporation, and Cy Green, the president of the Fred Meyer Corporation. Both of these men have impossible schedules—almost unimaginable demands on their time. Both returned my call within eight hours. Returning calls is a sign of responsibility and reliability.

Chapter 3

— E —

Extra Mile

"The extra mile has never had a traffic jam."

The "E" in Repeat stands for **extra mile**. One of the best ways to insure satisfied customers who give us repeat business is to go the extra mile. Unexpected, unanticipated services—the extras—more than pay their way in good will and prestige. Today's customers demand added value. They don't just **want** it, they **expect** it.

Marie Anderson, branch manager for U.S. Bank, told me, "I teach my employees that they are paid to provide courteous service. To me, going the extra mile is courtesy plus—above and beyond simple courtesy."

The Pedernales Electric Cooperative developed its Community Awareness Program in 1985. The purpose of the program was to improve relations between Pedernales and its customers. One part of the program involved equipping all company cars with two-way radios that could be used to radio for emergency road service. Another aspect was to train employees in first aid and

cardiopulmonary resuscitation. Much of Pedernales'
service area covers isolated, rugged terrain, and the
assistance provided by the company to rural customers has
saved several lives and has helped member customers think
of the cooperative as a neighbor rather than an impersonal
entity. This example of going the extra mile cost relatively
little while building customer loyalty.

The Mulcher

This past weekend I stopped at the lumber and
hardware department of a store I shop at frequently. I was
looking for a mulcher for chopping up limbs from our
yard. They didn't have one in stock. The manager, a
friendly, outgoing young man, asked if he could call
around for me. I said sure, if he didn't mind—it was a
busy Saturday. He grabbed the phone and started calling.
None could be found. To my surprise, a few days later he
called me at work and said he had a mulcher on layaway
for me at the Gresham store if I still wanted one.
"I sure do," I said. What a great example of going the
extra mile! Putting forth the extra effort made his
company a big sale—and a satisfied customer who will be
back for more—repeat business.

The Plane Ticket

Our daughter-in-law, Juliana Dennis, is the store
manager for a clothing specialty chain. She manages the
Walnut Creek, California store, fourth largest in a chain of
almost 100 stores. One of her customers recently moved
from Walnut Creek to Southern California. Soon after the
customer moved, her "personal buyer" came to Juliana and
asked if the store would transport the customer to Walnut

Creek to do some shopping. Juliana went the extra mile — she paid for the ticket. The customer flew to Walnut Creek and bought more than $13,000 worth of clothes that day. Going the extra mile pays off in big sales and creates satisfied, enthusiastic customers who go the extra mile to do business with you.

Mary's Place

While we were touring Ireland, celebrating our 25th wedding anniversary, we stopped to fill our rental car with petrol. It was late afternoon and we hadn't eaten since breakfast. We were ready for a late lunch/early dinner. I asked the attendant where in town we could find a good meal. Another customer who had just paid for his petrol said, in his wonderful Irish brogue, "Mary's is the place. Mary's is the only place. Will you be going there now? Oh, I'll take ye over. It's easier to take ye than to tell ye. Just follow me, I will show ye the way." And away we went. He was not only willing to tell us how to find Mary's, he was willing to lead us to the restaurant.

When we arrived in the little business section of town, the restaurant didn't look that impressive from the outside, certainly not by American standards. We walked inside and immediately felt the warmth of the old country decor with the fireplace and antiques all around. I had what I usually have—fish—and of course boiled Irish potatoes. The restaurant wasn't crowded and we started visiting with the couple sitting nearby. They were from Texas by way of New York and had come back to Ireland to retrace their roots. We had a marvelous meal and a wonderful time. I highly recommend "Mary's Place." We will always be grateful to the young man who went the extra mile to take us there.

No Room at the Inn

Later in the week, we were having a hard time finding a Bed and Breakfast Inn in Dublin because we had failed to phone ahead to make reservations. We stopped at a B & B in a northeast suburb. The lady of the house came to the door and said, "I'm sorry, we're all booked for the night, won't ye come in? Let me see what I can find for ye." She began calling around. She must have called six or eight B & B's before she was able to locate a place for us. She said, "It's only about ten blocks away but it can be a little confusing. I'll just take ye over." She backed her car out of the narrow driveway onto the cobblestone street and we followed her! When we got there she took us in, introduced us to the lady of the house and made sure that we were well cared for before she drove away. What a fabulous example of "going the extra mile!"

Closing Time

The next day we visited a factory outlet woolen shop. We couldn't decide on a couple of sweaters, so we left, and we returned at the end of the day. The manager was locking up the gate, closing out the cash register and finalizing all of the day's sales figures from the cash register. Still, they opened the door (a sliding door that looked like a rolling steel garage door) and said, "Come on in." They were very patient with us, and insisted that we take our time. It seems to me that everyone in Ireland has been through a course on customer relations and are experts on going the extra mile! We can't wait to go back, and we recommend Ireland as a great vacation destination.

Short Sleeves

Fred Stickel, president of Oregonian Publishing Company, told me about trying to get a special style dress shirt in size 16 x 32 from the downtown Portland Nordstrom store. The salesperson tried in the back room to find the shirt with no luck. She called all the Oregon stores—no shirt. She called the Washington stores—same result. She really went the extra mile, didn't she? But wait, she wasn't through yet! She said, "Mr. Stickel, I am very sorry. I will have our tailor shorten a 33 shirt's sleeves for you." Now that is going the extra mile for one less inch. How many people have heard this story of extraordinary service? What are you doing to provide extraordinary service—going the extra mile?

Wake Up Call

Earl and Pat Meyers recently returned from their wintering spot in Phoenix, Arizona. They were following their brother and sister-in-law, Art and Dorothy Dwyer, on their way back to Everett, Washington. Art and Dorothy said, "Let's stop at the Windmill in Roseburg, Oregon, for the night." It was apparent to Earl and Pat that Art and Dorothy had stopped there before.

The following morning, the wake-up was not the harsh ring of a phone, but instead a warm tap on the door. When Earl got up to open the door, he was greeted with hot coffee and fresh, warm donuts.

Art and Dorothy had been there before, and Earl and Pat are eager to go back. Going the extra mile doesn't have to cost a lot, it just has to show we care. It is amazing how much we appreciate the little things and how the little things can result in repeat business.

Grapefruit

Recently at lunch in Ellensburg, Washington, I asked the waiter for half a grapefruit. "I'm doing a little dieting." He said, "I'm sorry, we ran out earlier this morning. We do have some melon." He brought it, apologized for it being so small, and said he would give me a discount. I was there for almost two hours because our son was visiting one of our clients and I was doing some writing. The waiter came back several times and took good care of me.

"Can I get you anything else?"

"I sure wish you had a grapefruit," I said.

"Well, let me check again." It turned out that the kitchen did have grapefruits. The waiter brought me a beautiful juicy grapefruit. Extra Effort! He had been told there were none; he took the extra time to look for himself. That waiter earned a big tip!

Boots

Before Larry Jr. joined our firm he worked at a retail shoe store. One of his customers wanted a pair of boots that were on sale. Larry couldn't find them at his store in the color she wanted. It was a busy Saturday, and customers were waiting for help. Larry told her that he would call the other stores to check for the boots when the day slowed down. She gave him her name and telephone number and left. Around five o'clock he started calling other stores and eventually found the boots she wanted. He asked to have them sent to his store and called the customer to inform her of her good fortune! When the customer came in the next day to pick up her boots, she gave Larry a rose. She told him that other salespeople had taken her name and number but never called and she really appreciated his extra effort. From then on, she was one of Larry's best customers. Is it any wonder that he was able to personally sell over $250,000 worth of shoes a year before he was promoted to management?

A Moving Story

Not too long ago a woman friend, Marilyn told me her experience with transfer companies whom she had asked to move a desk from one room to another. Two companies thought she was ridiculous and responded: "We don't move desks." When she called a third company she said, "I don't know if you can help me or not, but this is not a joke. I'm serious about it." The receptionist answered, "If it's serious to you it's serious to me." Marilyn told her that she needed a desk moved and explained the details. "I can't do this," the receptionist said, "but I can have my manager call you. He'll be glad to help you." The manager called, the desk was moved, and after that Marilyn hired the company for three other moves. The desk move was $30; the next move was $850; the third $900, and the last, for her mother, was $750. Going the extra mile results in repeat business.

Bottle of Champagne

Another example of the extra mile was in the experience of Vicki Smith who was planning a buying trip to New York and knew she needed to leave early the following morning. She remembers the date very well because the following day was her birthday. She set her alarm early and went to bed for just a short nap.

The next thing she knew her daughter was shaking her and saying "Mother, I think you missed your flight." She had overslept. It was five minutes before her flight was supposed to leave. She had an advance-purchase ticket that couldn't be changed without substantial additional charges. She didn't know what to do. She called United Airlines, talked to three different people, gave them a very sad sob story. They agreed to make the change and even agreed to do it without charging the extra fees. She thanked them, mentioning she was especially grateful because it was her birthday.

When she got to the airport and encountered a different representative, she had some difficulty in getting the changes made.

"Well," she said, "your manager told me that I would be able to do it." Finally the change was made and she got her flight. When she arrived in New York she was greeted at the gate by a UAL passenger service representative who presented her with a bottle of champagne for her birthday.

That's a fabulous example of "going the extra mile." United Airlines could have made all the other changes and Vicki would have been a happy client. But by adding the champagne it was saying we value your patronage even if you have put us to a lot of extra trouble. By going the extra mile, United Airlines endeared itself to Vicki Smith and she will be flying extra miles with the airline.

Rain Man

Another example of the extra mile occurred recently when I was trying to rent a video movie. I never seem to do too well—I don't know what I want, I go late, and all of the new releases are out. I asked the young lady behind the counter if she had "Rain Man." She said, yes, there was one on hand but it was reserved. She asked me if I wanted her to call to see of the other customer still wanted it. I said sure, if she didn't mind. She quickly called. The customer said he had other plans for the evening. I got the movie because that video store clerk went the extra mile!

Million Dollar Parking

The failure to go the extra mile to extend small courtesies, can often be very expensive for the reluctant business. When John Barrier asked a Spokane bank teller last October to validate his parking ticket, the teller and the bank manager both refused because it was "against their policy."

Mr. Barrier withdrew his money, an estimated one million dollars, from the bank where he had done business for thirty years. He drove his pickup down the street to Seafirst, a competing bank, and opened a new account there. Seafirst featured the fifty-year old customer in its newsletter. He posed for a photo in front of his former bank, wearing his ordinary garb—sneakers and a grease-stained cap with Acme Concrete Co. above its bill. Seafirst's vice president for corporate affairs in Seattle confirmed the bank had a new client and said the story illustrated the importance of **every customer**.

The loss of Mr. Barrier as a customer has prompted his former bank to review the way it does business. How about you? Are there any little services your customers expect that you **refuse** to offer?

Spoon

Recently in our town a new supermarket opened. That's not an especially noteworthy event, but there was a lot of advertising and hoopla attending the opening. One of my secretaries visited the store and came back singing its praises. My wife and I decided to inspect the store for ourselves.

It turned out to be the most exciting retail grocery store I'd ever seen. There were small shops inside the store, a post office, a place to take your children. Pictures of all the department managers were proudly displayed. There was a customer service phone and hot line, in-store bakery, in-store deli, a place to sit and eat what you may have purchased from the bakery, deli, sandwich or salad bar while watching the news on a large screen television set. It was impressive.

The most impressive thing, however, happened when we were checking out. We had purchased a couple of yogurts to eat and after we paid for them I realized I had gotten only one spoon. I said to the young man who was about ready to take our groceries to the car, "I only got one spoon." He said, "Oh," and sprinted to the back of the store and was back in a flash with a second spoon and two napkins.

That single incident was more important to me than all the glamour and glitter of the beautiful new store. That kind of service inspires repeat business.

The Belt

Sometimes we have to do more than go the extra mile, we have to communicate to our customer that we have put out that extra effort. For example, a friend of mine took her sixteen-year-old son to Nordstrom in San Francisco to buy him a new suit—100% wool, first class. She bought him black leather shoes, socks, shirt, tie—the whole outfit. Unfortunately the store didn't have a black leather belt in his size. As the suit was being fitted, the saleslady said she would see what she could find. Ordinarily that would be the end of that, but the following day the mother received this phone call:

"Hello, Mrs. Anderson, this is Lisa from Nordstrom. I'm calling you from home. This is my day off and I took time this morning to do some shopping for you. I found a belt for your son. I located a good value over at Meier & Frank. They are holding it in your name."

This is how to make a life-long customer.

The extra mile is perception, and perception is everything. The customer must know you're putting forth extra effort. Whenever my Porsche needs a tune-up or other maintenance, I take it to Precision Auto. Fred, the owner and head mechanic, **always** does two or three extras, and notes them on the work order "no charge." If he didn't tell or show me, I'd never know he had gone the extra mile.

Recently I talked to Bill Borough, the manager of the Washington Square Nordstrom store, about a pair of pants I had taken in for alterations. I had lost my claim slip and he couldn't find any record on his computer of me ever bringing in the pants. I really had no recourse in this matter and certainly wouldn't have blamed him if he had said, "I'm sorry, Mr. Dennis, we can't do anything for you."

On the contrary, he said, "Come in and we'll replace your pants." I said, "That's not necessary." He said, "Please come in and let us replace your pants."

I said, "When I get some time, I'll try to stop by." He said, "No, don't wait until you have some time, I want you to come by. If we lost your pants, we are going to replace your pants!"

I did stop by about four weeks later. Bill remembered

the incident and set out to help me replace the missing pants. After that was done I started looking around. I ended up buying the first double-breasted suit I have owned for years, a Hickie Freeman sport coat, slacks, and six or eight neckties. Nordstrom more than made money by going the extra mile. It retained me as an enthusiastic, loyal customer, and each time I put on my free slacks my feeling for Nordie's is enhanced. Needless to say, this company has made me a loyal customer.

Shocking The Competition

An acquaintance of mine who works at U. S. Bank shared the following anecdote with me. It is a good example of going the extra mile.

An elderly bank customer decided to consolidate all of her business in one bank and requested U.S. Bank to cash out her certificate of deposit and to place the funds in First Interstate Bank. The U.S. Bank branch manager complied, himself going to her apartment for her to sign the withdrawal slip since she had difficulty walking. The manager personally took the bank's check to the other bank. When he casually gave the check to a customer service representative, he was asked what he did at his bank. Modestly, he said he was the branch manager. The customer service representative was shocked that a bank official with a high standing would perform such a mundane service. He was simply demonstrating what it means to go the extra mile.

Sheep Herder

In 1984, a big, dirty, four-wheel drive truck with sheep in the back pulled onto the Irwin Marina lot in Eugene,

Oregon. The driver, a sheep herder, looked around at some boats and ended up buying a 19-foot SeaRay Cutty Cabin for approximately $15,000. Jim Irwin stayed in touch with the customer and **"took care of him."** Three years later, the man returned and bought a $115,000 boat from Jim.

I asked Jim what he had done to **"take care"** of the customer in the three-year interim. He said he had gone out to the customer's house two or three times, showed him how to winterize his boat, and suggested little things about how to maintain it.

"Little things" go a long way toward creating loyal customers and **repeat business.**

Used Garage Door

People who understand about the extra mile turn up in all sorts of places. For example, I stopped at a lumberyard recently to ask about a garage door for an old shed on the back of my property. The company didn't sell garage doors.

The salesman said, "I used to be in the home improvement business and we got all of our garage doors from..." He gave me the name of the company.

"When I was in the home-improvement business," he said, "I had all kinds of used garage doors lying against my shed. They may have some used ones there, too." On a business card he wrote down the name of the company.

I really appreciated it—especially since it was about five o'clock and he was getting ready to close. I would have appreciated it even more if he had been able to give me the phone number.

Obviously, furnishing names and addresses of other stores wasn't his job or responsibility, yet it is that kind of extra effort we are all looking for that strengthens relationships, bonds customers, and keeps people coming back. It builds our repeat business. As a result of his suggestion, I was able to eventually find a used garage door for my old lower shed for thirty-five dollars. I feel obligated to him and his company. He will see me again for repeat business.

Mount Success Seminar

Jesus of Nazareth was teaching a success seminar, commonly referred to as "The Sermon on the Mount" or the "Be-attitudes"—attitudes for being successful. He was talking about successful living, and his suggestion was: "...and if any one forces you to go one mile, go with him two miles." — Matthew 5:41, RSV

Evidence reveals that Jesus's suggestion may not have been enthusiastically received. The Jews Jesus was talking to were under the domination of the Romans and were required by law to carry the Roman Soldiers' armor, duffle bag, and equipment for a mile upon request. Roman roads were marked off by mile markers.

Can't you just see how they picked up the duffle bag, carried it grumbling all the way, and plunked it down at the exact end of one mile? Jesus' admonition was that if you were compelled to go a mile, go two. On one level, it seems so unfair and so unjust and so unlikely to be a key to success. There is a kind of conventional wisdom that says we should do less, see how little we can get by with, do the bare minimum. The Be-attitudes as expressed by Jesus suggested that we do more. Do more than we're asked to do, do more than we're paid to do, and in so doing, achieve real success.

- What are you doing to provide extraordinary service?
- What is your plan for going the extra mile?

Chapter 4

— P —

Pleasant Personality

*"Life is not so short but that there is always
time enough for courtesy."*

Ralph Waldo Emerson

Smile

The first sign of a **pleasant personality** is a smile. A
Chinese proverb says, "Man without a smile should not
open shop." When I began conducting sales training
classes over 20 years ago, my wife managed the
administrative affairs at the back of the room. Often she
would make an 8 x 11 sign, **SMILE,** and tape it to the table
for me to see. I was so intent on my job of teaching that I
forgot to smile. I had to train myself to smile. When I am
speaking I find myself looking for smiling faces. I guess I
need the encouragement of audience approval and
acceptance. A smile reassures me, makes me feel welcome,
appreciated, builds my confidence. I loved my job as a
sales course instructor, but it isn't enough to like people
and what we are doing. We need to show it. And one of the

easiest, best ways to do it is with a warm, sincere smile. A smile is like a light in the window that says "Welcome Home," a sign of friendship. A smile happens in a split second, but the memory can last forever.

Being courteous to everyone you meet begins with a desire to please, and what is so exciting is when we want to please, others respond in kind and are naturally eager to please. Poor manners show incompetence and arrogance. Don't forget the Golden Rule. Treat your customers and fellow employees as you would want to be treated. Extending a little courtesy to someone might cause them to say, "That person is doing a good job. She is an asset to the company." Courtesy always draws positive attention to you.

Look for ways to compliment and praise your customers on their choice in merchandise. I love it when the waiter says to me after I have ordered, "Good choice." This morning I stopped at my favorite stop on my way to Seattle. Isn't it interesting how we've all developed our "favorite stop." Have you ever wondered why you keep going back to that "favorite stop?" Maybe it has escaped you consciously, maybe it has even escaped you subconsciously. But my stop represents repeat business for a particular gas station and convenience store.

On a very tight schedule this morning, I ran in quickly to the restroom, came back out, got a cup of tea in my thermos container and went to check out. The attendant said, "Sixteen cents." That may be why I keep going back. That's quite a surprise.

As I was trying to get my change together, still somewhat blurry-eyed at 6:00 in the morning, she said, "That's a great tie!"

Her comment sparked me up, made my day. Since I had taken some time to pick out the tie—it went well with the shirt and suit I had on—the compliment reassured me and built my confidence as I drove on to Seattle. It is remarkable how important the little things in life can be. A compliment can change your day, have pleasant repercussions far beyond the original intent.

Friendliness Helps Pump 300,000 Gallons

What can an attitude of friendliness do? Last Monday Larry, Jr. and I had a cup of coffee with Nancy Rayner, a recent graduate of our Leadership LAB. Nancy was recently divorced, had no real business training, and was the first woman franchisee for an AM/PM Mini-Market. Nancy's story is one of the most exciting I've heard from the thousands of people I've met and interviewed.

Nancy took over an AM-PM store four years ago. At the time her store was pumping about 70 thousand gallons of gas a month. She knew she had to raise the gallonage in order to make the payments on her store. Nancy was committed to a degree of success that had never been achieved before. She began to do a lot of small things that endeared her to her customers, but there was one thing that proved to be the most effective in boosting her sales. They went from 70,000 to 100,000, then from 150,000 to 300,000 gallons a month—her big goal. Nancy's secret was to personally **stay on the floor and greet her customers. She remembered their names, greeted them individually, and trained her employees to do the same.**

Small things work! Nancy's Mini-Mart in Union Gap competes favorably with bigger stores in Seattle. It is the number two store in the state—all because she knows the value of friendliness.

Appearance

Businesses take on the personalities of the people who run them. One of the ways we judge a persons personality is by his or her appearance. The same principle applies to a business. A few months ago, I pulled into a truck stop. It was the kind we have all visited with popcorn and pop in the self-serve containers, baseball caps, belt-buckles, and audio cassettes that truckers buy.

The young lady who waited on me was down on her hands and knees, when I encountered her, scraping out the tiny bit of dirt between the cove molding on the floor and the floor tile itself. I seldom see this attention to detail and cleanliness.

Since all of us generalize from one observation the entire impression of a business, I concluded the store was spic and span. In the same way you'll judge the efficiency of an airplane when you get to your seat and find the service tray won't stay up. You ask the attendant for help and she says, "I guess you'll have to hold it up for takeoff." By her answer you may conclude that the whole plane is falling apart and soon an engine will fall off the wing. Attention to detail and cleanliness smacks of order and quality. I am more willing, eager, and likely to do repeat business with an organization that's neat, clean, and well kept.

Fish Story

I met my brother Bruce at a restaurant this spring. I asked the waitress about the fish special. Instead of the perfunctory answer I am accustomed to, the waitress replied, "It's fresh trout, and it's never been frozen. It comes with your choice of potato—fries, wedges, mashed, or baked, a buttermilk biscuit or a blueberry bran muffin, and some fresh vegies and a dinner salad or a cup of soup." After I placed my order she said, "We also have fresh strawberry pie, and chocolate peanut butter pie is our pie of the day." Here was that rare person who knows how to serve, enjoyed her job, added to the whole dining experience of the customer and gently cross-sold the customers with her dessert suggestions.

Peddler

Brian Cole of Yakima, Washington is an avid cyclist. He owns a very expensive mountain bike and gives it the best care and upkeep possible. Brian told me he will not buy parts and accessories from a local bike shop because the owner and employees seem aloof, stuck-up, and snobbish. Instead, Brian drives forty minutes to Ellensburg to buy parts for his bike. I am not quite sure what Brian means by snobbish—I've never visited that shop—but Brian's story makes the point that a pleasing personality is a must for repeat business.

Signs of a courteous person include cheerfulness, tact, patience, cooperation, and respect. Little words such as "Please" and "Thank You" often matter more than many big words. Success in any business will come only through developing relationships. We go further faster if we make a point of being courteous and friendly with our customers **and** the people we work with.

The Extra Key

If an example were ever needed on how not to treat a customer, the anecdote that follows, related by Clyde Betts, is an outstanding one: "While visiting a local shopping center with my wife and mother-in-law, I saw a sale sign in the window of a large, national chain store advertising keys made for seventy-nine cents. My daughter had just lost her keys so I decided to have some house and car keys made. When I returned to the car and tried the new key, it wouldn't work. I said jokingly, "That must be why they are on sale."

My mother-in-law told me to go back to the store and tell them to make it right. I went back and they cut another key. I returned to the car and the second key didn't work either. My mother-in-law said, "Go get your money back."

I said it wasn't worth the effort and time for seventy-nine cents.

She insisted, "It's not the money, it's the principle of the thing."

I returned to the key-maker and told her the key didn't work and I wanted my money back.

She said "If you want your money back, you have to go upstairs to customer service."

I went upstairs, found the customer service department, and stood in line. It was more important to keep my mother-in-law happy and get the money than prove my point.

The lady at customer service would not take the bad key back. She told me to go to the key-maker and get a refund slip. I was really getting the run around. I went back downstairs and got a refund slip. I then went back upstairs and stood in line again. When it was my turn the lady said in a loud voice, "You would do anything for seventy-nine cents, wouldn't you?" She threw the change in the tray and said, "Next."

I felt insulted, humiliated, and angry. I will never give this store another chance to get my business. When I got back to the car, my wife smiled and said, "Well, did you get your money?"

I looked at my mother-in-law and grinned. I then proceeded to tell my wife that it's not the money, "It's the principle of the thing."

Imagine how many times the story of the key will be told to the detriment of the chain store whose reputation will be injured with every repetition. The harm done is incalculable. If the store is so callous about a small thing like a key, what must its policies be about bigger things? This is the question an offended customer asks himself. A customer will go out of his way to tell his story of outrage.

Almost nothing surprises me anymore when I'm shopping in mass-merchandise stores. But I do have to admit I was at least a little shocked when I witnessed the following: a customer paid for a $3.98 purchase with a handful of dimes. "There's $2.00," he said and began to count out the balance. The saleslady's astonishing response was "Yuck!" The customer asked, "What's yuck?" and she said, "All those dimes." He said, "It's money, isn't it? What's your name?" I don't blame him for asking for her name. He went on to reprimand her and told her she had a poor attitude.

It was embarrassing for me standing nearby and certainly embarrassing for the saleslady and the other customers standing around. I had observed her earlier. She simply did not know how to perform customer service. Perhaps she was a person who was untrainable in that job, but certainly management had the responsibility to monitor her behavior and replace her. While she received the brunt of the customer's criticism, it was the store that inherited the residue of the customer's resentment for hiring her.

A study conducted for the White House Office of Consumer Affairs indicates that 96 percent of customer complaints are never voiced. However, the quick resolution of a customer complaint will retain the customer and will be advertised by word-of-mouth. Document your customers' complaints. These records can be used to monitor consumer trends, develop (or revise) product lines and services to become more competitive, and to discern the real reason customers stop coming back.

The White House Study indicated that negative stories are created when customers perceive that they have received service of less value than they expected and:

- On average, each customer will tell a negative story to nine other people.

- Thirteen percent of the disgruntled customers will tell twenty or more people about their experience.

Actually, this negative effect is compounded because no one tells the same story nine times without embellishing it to get a better reaction from an audience. By the time a story is told the ninth time, it can be so exaggerated as to be unfair and misleading. This is unfortunate, because a negative story is two times more likely to be told than a positive one.

Technical Assistance Research Programs, Inc. (TARP), which conducted the White House Study, also produced information that indicated that:

- Seventy percent of disgruntled customers will return if the company apologizes for an error.

- Ninety-five percent will return if the front line employee impressively recovers.

The TARP research demonstrated that customers who complain are more likely to return—even if they receive nothing more than an apology. The clear financial implication is that if you make it easy for customers to complain, even if the company does not recover well, the company has increased its chances of getting repeat business. Adding a positive recovery strategy to a method of discovering unhappy customers increases the repeat business factor even more.

Customers are tired of complaining only to be told that they have the right company but the wrong person. Any person in the "right company" should react in a way that effectively resolves the customer's problem. Playing "interdepartmental ping-pong" just frustrates everyone. There is nothing more stressful or frustrating to the customer than being bounced around from department to department. Use your creativity and good judgement to resolve problems.

Resolve the service problems you find rather than passing them to someone else. Don't pass the buck. One night I returned a pair of shoes to a store that had a great reputation for accepting anything back with which the customer is dissatisfied. When a salesman approached me and asked me how he could be of help, I said, "I have a pair of shoes here I'm one hundred percent dissatisfied with." So we took them out of the bag and he asked, "What's wrong with them?"

In a very conversational tone I said, "They squeak."

He asked, "What would you like for us to do?"

I responded, "Let's see what we can trade them in on."

It's not comfortable for the average customer to return merchandise. So when you encounter such a customer it's important to remember that the customer is carrying an emotional load and is probably under stress, ready to be defensive. My salesman reduced my emotional load by asking the question, "What would you like for us to do." He demonstrated several pairs of shoes. He knew his merchandise and he recommended a pair that he wore when he was on his feet for a long time.

Handling Complaints

Since the TARP research indicated that negative stories are twice as likely to be told as positive stories, a company's goal must be to eliminate negative stories wherever possible. When mistakes do occur, you must recover in a way that so impresses the customer that he feels better about your service than if you had not made the mistake in the first place.

An unhappy customer is an opportunity. In fact, it may be the best opportunity to create a positive story. When a customer becomes frustrated, he expects less from a company in the future. You can impress a customer strongly if you acknowledge your mistake, empathize with the customer's concern, and take immediate action to resolve the problem.

Recovery situations actually provide an opportunity to be magnificent. They may be the best way to communicate the company's reliability, empathy toward its customers, and willingness to "customize" the experience for every customer.

How far should you go to please an angry customer? Whatever it takes. A single complainer left unhappy can damage your business faster than you can say, "Sorry about that." Studies show that customers tell **four times** as many people about bad experiences as good ones. Sure it might cost you a few bucks. But it costs far more to **replace** a customer than to **keep** one. Why spend money attracting new, sometimes unprofitable customers while valuable existing customers walk off in a huff?

When problems arise, the best service organizations recover and handle the customer's issues, concerns, and problems better than their competition. They make recovery hassle-free. They don't put the customer through a complex maze of steps. They take responsibility for the customer's experience and find a way to solve problems in an easy to do, business-like manner.

Great service organizations realize that many dissatisfied customers won't complain about service issues. Accordingly, a well-administered, customer recovery process will generate the type of information that is needed to improve the service process. The reasons customers complain must be recorded and routinely audited in order to find trends.

Customer complaints are the school books from which we learn. We must keep asking our customers, "Is our service satisfying? Do you have any complaints, comments, or suggestions?"

A hardware store in the midwest is so sure complainers are an important source of information about how it can improve its service that it sends its complaining customers a bouquet of roses.

According to *Target Marketing Magazine*, proper handling of consumer inquiries can build loyalty and promote sales for direct marketers. A Technical Assistance Research Institute study found that 70 percent of customers who have problems when ordering through direct-marketing channels never complain; they simply stop ordering. Among consumers who do complain, nearly 70 percent purchasing items costing $100 or less continue their relationship with the firm when their complaints are handled satisfactorily.

The five most common causes of customer complaints are: poor quality of service; damaged products; incorrect products shipped to customers; limited selection of products available, and unprofessional sales personnel. The most effective way to resolve a customer complaint is to stay calm and respond quickly.

Cup of Coffee

That's what happened when my wife discovered that her favorite brand of coffee had been replaced at our neighborhood store where she shops. She complained to the store manager who referred her to the buyer. She called the buyer at the corporate headquarters and he referred her complaint call to the company that was now installing its coffee in the store.

That new coffee company sent her a beautiful letter acknowledging her complaint and expressing its desire that she would learn to enjoy its brand of coffee as much, if not more, than the brand she'd been buying. Along with the response letter came three pounds of the company's gourmet blends. It was an extraordinary way to respond to a consumer complaint about an insignificant thing like a change in brand of coffee.

Was it such a small complaint after all? I don't know how much money the average person spends in a grocery store in a year. My guess is that in the case of our household it's right around $7,000. No small purchase. It's like buying a new car every year without a trade-in. The store manager was smart, acted in a wise manner when he referred my wife's complaint to his supplier. And that supplier acted wisely when it sent my wife the letter and free coffee sample and sent a copy of the correspondence to the store manager.

Cold Shoulder

Contrast the coffee company's response to a complaint with the cold shoulder I got at a restaurant.

A restaurant where I stopped for lunch was cold. I verified the fact with a woman who sat in the booth next to me. "It sure is. It's always cold in here."

I went to the manager and said, "It's cold in here." He didn't look up, didn't look at me. I asked if he had heard me. He said, "Yes, I'll try to get to it when I'm not so busy."

Thirty minutes later, after both my neighbor and I had complained to a couple of other persons in the restaurant, someone finally turned the heat up a little bit. This was, of course, an example of keeping the restaurant comfortable for the help who are in the kitchen instead of keeping the temperature comfortable for the customers.

I hurriedly wrote a note on the comments card about the restaurant being cold, about how the manager responded, and said simply I wouldn't be returning. I haven't heard from the restaurant's headquarters and doubt that I will. And I *won't* be a repeat customer.

A couple of weekends ago, when our Sunday paper came, the insert, *Parade Magazine*, was very poorly printed. There was a big black smudge on part of a page. The smudge was on part of an article I found interesting, and I wanted to be able to read it. For the first time in my 15 years as a subscriber to the paper, I called to ask for a second copy of the insert to be mailed to our home. As I knew the publisher, I talked to his executive secretary who transferred me to the customer service department hotline where I explained my request. The young lady who answered the phone said, "You should have called us yesterday. We have an 800 number you can call anytime the paper is delivered incorrectly or the paper is not correct. We'll <u>try</u> to get another one out to you later this week."

There was no apology. She did not give me the 800

number. She told me what I "should do," and told me that she would try. This was one of my worst experiences with a complaint. I don't blame the young lady who answered the phone. I blame her supervisors, managers, and I blame her training program, if there was one.

Handling complaints takes particular care and effort, especially if you are dealing directly with the public. The points offered here represent the collected wisdom of a lot of companies which treat complaints as valuable estimates of how well they are taking care of their customers:

1. **Remember** that your instinctive reaction to someone who starts to "chew you out" is to get pretty huffy yourself. Of course, that's the worst thing you can do.

2. **Control your temper** if you hope to control the situation. Keep your voice calm and matter of fact and your manner attentive and helpful. Deliberately slow down your pace of speaking and drop your volume of speech a few decibels. Respond to the message. Don't react to the messenger's treatment. Don't argue or contradict.

3. **Show concern immediately.** Delay just compounds the problem. Use appropriate open body posture. Don't frown or scowl.

4. **Learn the customer's name and use it.** Treat the complainer as an individual, make him feel special.

5. **Listen attentively and patiently.** Pay attention. Let the customer talk. Ask questions even if you have heard the complaint hundreds of times. Listen as if you never heard the complaint before. Say to yourself, "This is the most interesting thing I have ever heard." Use calming statements like, "I understand how you must feel." Taking notes is another way of showing concern. Get all the facts. Agree, if you can, without being misleading. Let the complainer see that you understand why he is "burning"

and, if appropriate, side with his anger without criticizing your company or other departments or suppliers.

6. Don't interrupt, don't butt in. Interrupting the complainer implies that you think his complaint isn't valid. Let him talk himself out.

7. Restate the complaint as you understand it. This shows you were listening and makes sure both of you agree on the basis for the complaint.

8. Qualify your requests with the reason for asking. "So that I can go right to the trouble spot, may I have your account number?"

9. Thank the person for complaining to you. Be glad the complainant spoke to you instead of talking about his grievance to other people. Express your appreciation to him for making the complaint. Remember, he could stop doing business with you and become a negative commercial. In fact, research indicates that dissatisfied customers only tell us four percent of the time. Ninety-six percent of our unhappy customers *never* tell us.

10. Acknowledge the strong feelings your customer may have. "I know how frustrating it is to have to wait..."

11. Apologize for any trouble and inconvenience he has experienced.

12. If you or your company are at fault, admit it quickly—don't dwell on it. Nothing will lower an angry customer's temperature faster than honest acknowledgement of an error.

13. Do everything you can to correct the trouble that produced the storm. If immediate action is impossible, let him know that the matter will be acted on promptly and that he will be advised.

14. Offer a generous settlement. When the customer has calmed down, ask, "What would you like to have me do?" Often it is less than you would have offered. When you can offer more or offer an appropriate alternative to what the customer expects, it's a good investment in future business. If the complaint requires a follow-up, tell him exactly when you will be back in touch. Avoid "we will try," "I will try" —make a commitment. This shows sincerity and relieves the tension.

15. **Spell out your action step.** "...let's arrange our schedules for when you'll be coming back so we can be available for you." Give the number of steps you will need to solve the problem. "We need to do three things to solve this problem." Keep selling. While the customer is pleased with your handling of the complaint, why not suggest additional ways you can be of service.

16. **When, while endeavoring to solve a problem you find the answer**, say, "I found the answer," "I have what you need," "I have the help you need." Speak with excitement, enthusiasm, pick up your pace of speaking and speak with greater animation and volume than you customarily speak. This will communicate your sincere interest, your sincere desire, your excitement in having been able to serve your customer.

By following these guidelines for applying a pleasing personality to complaints, you will turn upsets into up-sales.

So how about it? Is every customer really worth saving? We all get cranky, hot, tired—that's understandable. But let's face it, some people can be a royal pain. Studies by Technical Assistance Research Programs (TARP) of Washington, DC suggest that up to 30 percent of problems result from customer errors or product misuse. And inevitably there are people who are just plain mean. Some customers belittle, demand, threaten harm, lie, rant, and rave. Should they be handled differently? Some people think being obnoxious is the only way to get action. When you are professional, firm, and pleasant in response, they often calm down in a hurry. Listen, don't interrupt. Take notes. Show genuine concern. Be calm and give the impression of confidence. That will help put you in control without appearing arrogant.

Some people take advantage of a "satisfaction guaranteed" policy, bring back clothes they've worn, a hair dryer they didn't buy from you, the can opener they damaged by misuse. Smile and express regret the product or service failed to satisfy. Remember, for every sour apple, there are 99 good ones. Patience will pay off. My experience with a bad meal but a superlative waitress exemplifies patience and the right attitude.

Cold Fish

Not too long ago on a Sunday, after church, my wife and I stopped at a restaurant for lunch. I'd eaten at the same restaurant chain a few days earlier in another location and had ordered their "All-you-can-eat" fish basket. I said to the waitress, "I think I'll have the 'All-you-can-eat fish basket' again, but when I had it the other day, I wasn't really satisfied with the way the fish was prepared."

Her response, in a warm, friendly way, was "But I'll bet you didn't have me as your waitress, did you?"

I thought to myself, "What a wonderful way to handle a complaint." The truth is, the meal wasn't much better than the first one. In fact, I'll never have it again. But the waitress handled the complaint and all of our service in such a gracious, warm, friendly, enthusiastic way that I may go back there to see if I can get her as my waitress again.

Names

Another example of a pleasant personality is using the customer's name. The theme song for the long-running television show "Cheers" is "Where everybody knows your name." It is true, we love to hear our name spoken; it gives us a sense of importance and we go back to the place that knows us by name.

Do you recall when you met someone new, and when they saw you a few days later they greeted you by your name? Did it make you feel good? You bet it did! Employees, wives, husbands, friends, customers— everybody wants to be remembered. Have you noticed when you call a customer's kids or spouse by name after you have taken his credit card or check, that he is usually pleasantly surprised—even shocked? People don't expect those with whom they are not close to remember who they are. When it happens, they feel special because you have singled them out for individual attention. As a result they will listen more closely to what you have to say.

In almost every city in the world, you can find monuments to people who want to be remembered. They wanted it so badly they laid out plans to be immortal. Andrew Carnegie's name will never die. Only yesterday I heard his name on the news as a report was being given about the research of the Andrew Carnegie Foundation for the advancement of teaching. Every year in America people donate hundreds of millions of dollars to colleges, hospitals, churches and other organizations, with the provision that a wing, room, or building be named after them. Hundreds of educational institutions all over the world were founded because people wanted to be remembered. The noted Rockefeller and Ford Foundations with their branches in every country in the world are memorials to men who wanted to be remembered. In Portland, Oregon, Arlene Schnitzer donated a million dollars to complete the renovation of the Civic Theater. Consequently, the theater was renamed the Arlene Schnitzer Concert Hall.

Last week I visited with the editor of an in-company publication. She was fielding a call from one of the employees of the company who had misunderstood an article in the company paper. This person raged on about the way the article had been written. The editor did a fine job of fielding the complaint. After the conversation was finally over, I suggested to the editor that in the future she use the complainer's name several times when responding to the complaint. She thought about it a second and said yes, that would help to calm them down.

My friend, Jack Root, president of Money Management Systems, was standing in the Memphis, Tennessee airport when a man walked up and said, "Jack Root, how are you?" Jack was shocked and impressed. Jack had met the man three years earlier—a brief meeting that lasted fifteen or twenty minutes. He gained new respect and admiration for the man all because his name had been remembered.

The Advantages of Remembering Names

The best way to gain a person's favorable attention is to use that person's name. Memory, particularly when it comes to someone's name, is a powerful tool. If you are like most people you have a lazy memory. Some things you remember easily, without any effort it seems. Other things you find practically impossible to remember, try as hard as you will. You take for granted that your memory is poor and you do nothing about it.

In our work all over America thousands of people have told us that they have a poor memory—especially for names. This is not true as they have proven to themselves many times. Hundreds of times we have shown a group of fifty or sixty people who have never seen each other before how they can remember each other's names at least ninety percent of the time. We not only showed them, they did it! The advantages of remembering names are:

1. Gaining confidence.
2. Appearing more professional.
3. Widening our circle of friends.
4. Helping people be more receptive to us and our ideas.
5. Leading by example—what would we like others to do for us? *Remember us and our names.*

The disadvantages of forgetting names are:

1. Embarrassment.
2. Appearing unprofessional
3. Appearing aloof.
4. Withdrawing from conversations and groups.
5. Showing a lack of caring concern.

Why Don't We Remember Names?

First, we don't recognize how important names are. Second, we don't know how to remember names. The truth is we can remember names. It requires effort, organization, and commitment. Like any other skill—cross-country skiing, mountain climbing, bicycling—improved memory comes from consistent, determined effort and practicing correct techniques.

A Good Memory is Easy

A poor memory is a disadvantage and exacts a heavy toll from us in a thousand ways. A little understanding, a little effort, and a little game transforms a supposedly poor memory into an unusually good memory within a month and often within only a week. We have seen it happen thousands of times. It's a game, it's fun. You'll enjoy every minute of it.

Here are some ideas to help you remember names:

Attention is Magic

Some things you remember easily. Did you ever stop to ask yourself why? The reason is—you give attention. You are interested and want to remember. But sometimes you think you give attention when you really don't. Consider the people you were introduced to the other day. Yes, in a mild way you wanted to remember their names but when you were introduced to them, what were you thinking? Nine times out of ten you were thinking about yourself—what kind of an impression you were making, whether or not your clothes look good, what you were going to eat for dinner. You weren't thinking about the people or their names. If you had been, you would have remembered easily.

Act on Your Ideas

Until the new memory system you learn here is linked with appropriate action and consistent practice you won't really benefit. Since it only takes a few weeks of practice to become very good at always remembering people's names jump, right in and practice as often as you can throughout each day.

Newspapers, magazines, and television offer many opportunities to practice connecting names with faces. Within days you'll form the habit of using your memory skills at each new meeting. Soon you'll find yourself automatically remembering the name of every new person you meet. You'll have a powerful, valuable ability that will serve you for the rest of your life!

<u>Pictures Work</u>

We have learned that the mind "sees" pictures more vividly than it remembers concepts. When you take the time to use pictures to remember someone's name your memory increases one hundred percent. Make your picture immediately. Use that wonderful imagination to link a person's name with an active, clear picture. The few seconds it takes to picture Mary Johnson laughing **merrily** while wearing her **son's longjohns** will save hours of searching your memory for her name when you next meet! In other words, form mental PICTURES. Here are seven ideas that will help you "PICTURE," and as a result, remember customers' names easily, quickly, and permanently.

Pause for a moment when you hear a name or meet a new person. Stop thinking about yourself, the conversation, and the world around you. For ten seconds think of nothing but the person you just met, <u>who</u> he is and **his name.**

Image - The tool you can use every time to remember names is visualization. Visualize the person doing something that depicts his/her name. Use a vivid, mental image with color. Exaggerate. As you gain experience creating visual images for people's names, you'll develop a knack for quickly thinking of images that will help you connect their face with their name. Your images don't need to make sense to anyone else. Make them humorous, full of action—whatever makes them memorable to you.

Clear Impression - Form a clear impression of the person and a clear impression of his name. So often we don't really hear the name because it is said so fast or slurred. Pay the person a compliment: ask him to repeat his name or spell it, and get the proper pronunciation.

Think of someone you know with a similar name. When I met Bruce Beauchamp it was easy for me to remember his name because my brother's name is Bruce. Associate people and their names with someone else you know, or something else they remind you of. Associate the new with the old, the odd, or the ridiculous.

Understand the National Origin - Being aware of the national origin or commenting on the nationality of a persons name helps to strengthen the impression, making retention easier. Does the name have a meaning that can help you remember it, like Carpenter, Smith, Jewel, Mason, Hunter? My friend, Dr. Tom Ashlock's, forebears came from England where they made locks from ash.

Rhyme by its nature helps a concept stick in our minds. We remember poems, lyrics to songs, and commercials easily because of rhyme.

Enthusiasm—Any new skill that requires breaking old habits and old behaviors is tough. The way to compensate for that difficulty is to use an extra measure of enthusiasm. Your name is so important to you that your mind literally short circuits when you hear it—and so do the minds of others when they hear their names.

Developing skill at remembering names is like developing any other skill; at first it is hard but the longer you work at it, the easier it gets. Have fun with it and you will be proud of yourself.

The following are suggested mind pictures you may want to use for common names.

Larry	— Twirling a lariat
Dennis	— Sitting in a dentist's chair
Adam	— Big Adam's apple
Alan	— Allen wrench

Amy	— Aim at target
Andrew	— Drawing a picture
Barbara/Barb	— Wrapped in barbed wire
Barry	— Picking berries
Ben	— Big Ben
Betty	— Betting with a deck of cards
Beverly	— Beverage
Bill	— Big-billed cap
Bob	— Bobbing for apples
Bruce	— Big bruise on his chin
Carl	— Driving in a car - L for Lincoln
Carol	— Caroling
Cheryl	— Sharing L's
Christine/Chris	— Kris Kringle
Chuck	— Throwing it away
Dan	— Daniel in the lion's den
David	— With a sling to kill Goliath
Dawn	— Dawn coming over the horizon
Debbie	— Debutante
Dick	— Private eye with collar up
Don	— Don Juan
Donna	— Dawning
Doris	— Doors
Doug	— Digging a hole (past tense)
Ed	— The talking horse
Eileen	— Eye leaning or I-beam
Elizabeth	— Lizard
Ellen	— Island
Frank	— Frankfurter

Fred	— Frayed
Gail	— Strong wind
Gary	— Gary, Indiana
George	— Gorge
Gloria	— Glow or Old Glory
Gordon	— Out working in the garden
Greg	— Keg
Harry	— Hair all over
Helen	— Helmet
Holly	— Boughs of holly or holy
Jack	— Jacking up a car
James	— Jesse
Jean	— Blue jeans
Jeff	— Chef
Jim	— In gym pressing weights
Joan	— Joan of Arc
John	— Sitting on toilet
Joe	— G. I. Joe
Joyce	— Juice
Judy	— Judo
Karen	— Caring person, nurse
Kathleen/Kathy	— Petting a kitty
Lee	— Wearing Levi's
Linda	— Lint
Lucy	— Loose
Mark	— Mark on his forehead
Mary	— Bride
Mike	— Holding a microphone
Nancy	— Fancy
Neil	— On his knees
Nick	— Neck or nickel
Nicole	— Nickel
Pamela	— Pan
Patricia/Pat	— Pats of butter

Paul	— Pole
Peggy	— Peg
Philip	— Full lip or Phillips screwdriver
Rachel	— Ratchet
Ralph	— Rough or throw up
Ray	— Ray of sunshine
Richard	— Rich heart
Rick	— Pulling a rickshaw
Robert	— Robber
Roger	— Roger, over, and out
Ronald	— Run
Rose	— Rose
Roxanne	— Rocks, hand
Sam	— Uncle Sam
Sandy/Sandra	— Sand
Scott	— Scott towel - Kilts
Steve	— Stevedore pushing a carton
Susan	— Lazy susan
Ted	— Teddy bear
Theresa/Terry	— Trees or terry towel
Tim	— Timer
Todd	— Toddler
Tom	— Tom-tom drum
Tony	— Toe coming out of his knee
Vicki	— Rubbing Vicks Vapo-Rub
Wanda	— Wand
Willina	— She will learn

Last Names

Anderson	— With their son
Armstrong	— Strong arm

Baker	— Baker or bakery
Barrett	— Barrette or beret
Bennett	— Bonnet
Black	— Blackboard or blackjack
Blacksmith	— Beating on an anvil
Bowen	— A bow and arrow
Brainich	— Brain is itchy
Brewster	— Brew or brewery
Brown	— Brown color or brownie
Burns	— Burner or sideburns
Campbell	— Camp, or camper
Carey	— Carrying a lot of...
Clark	— Clark bar
Cook	— Chef with hat on
Davis	— Davis Cup
Eagan	— Eagle
Evans	— Ovens
Foster	— Frosting
Gallagher	— Galloper or gallery
Grant	— Granite
Green	— Greenhouse or golf green
Hamilton	— A large ham
Harris	— Hairs
Hayzlett	— Eating hazel nuts
Henderson	— Hen, doors with son
Hoagland	— Land of hogs, hog pen
Hoffman	— Half-moon
Holthe	— Hole in the bow of a ship
House	— In a big house
Huber	— Hues of color, rainbow
Jackson	— Car jack or Jack with son
Johnson	— Toilet with son
Jones	— Bones or cones
Kaufman	— Cough or cuff

Kelly	— Jelly
Kennedy	— Can of tea
Knutson	— Canoe with son
Kortekass	— A quart of gas
Kramer	— Creamer
Lawson	— Police officer, judge with son
Leach	— Killing a leech with bleach
Lockhart	— A padlock on the heart
Lynch	— Lynching or noose
Marshall	— Marshal or big star on chest
McDonald	— Ronald McDonald
McLoughlin	— Laughing into a microphone
Meyers	— Stuck in the mire or mirrors
Miller	— Mill or miller
Moore	— Mower
Murphy	— Mercy, mercury, or murky
Neilson	— Kneeling with son
Newman	— New man wearing sales tags
Noll	— A knoll or rolling hills
Norris	— Nurse
Oakley	— Oak tree leaning with leaves
O'Brien	— Brain
Paige	— Page of a book or magazine
Parker	— Parking meter
Patterson	— Patting son on head
Pearson	— Pear or pier with son

Powers	— Power tool or towers
Preston	— Pressed
Rogers	— Rod, jars
Russell	— Wrestle
Scott	— Skid
Shay	— Shade
Simpson	— Shrimp or Sampson
Smith	— Blacksmith
Steele	— Steel bar or pipe
Stewart	— Stew or steward
Swanson	— Swam with little swan
Taylor	— Tail or tailor with scissors
Thomas	— Beating on a tom-tom at Mass
Thompson	— Tom-tom drum with son
Ternan	— Tears coming from the man
Tucker	— Trucker or car
Wagner	— Wagon
Walker	— Baby walker
Washington	— Washing machine
Webb	— Caught in a cobweb
Weed	— In the weeds
West	— Vest or 10-gallon hat
Williams	— Well full of yams
Wilson	— Whistle
Wright	— Turning right

You will develop a knack for creating your own mind pictures to match with names once you get in the habit of doing the exercise. And you'll be surprised at the added attention you get from people who are pleased that you remembered their favorite words—their own names.

More About Names

After one of my classes, I stopped off at the Newport Bay restaurant to visit with an associate and have a cup of soup. When the waiter, whom I had known for a while, gave me my bill, he said, "Thank you, Mr, Dennis." As we were leaving the restaurant, he called out, "Have a pleasant evening, Mr. Dennis." He made it a point to use my name twice. Look for and find out your customer's name. Then use his name from the beginning and use it often.

Because of my hectic schedule, it seems difficult for me to stop and get a haircut as often as I'd like. I recently found myself getting a haircut in a mall in central Washington. I walked into the hair-styling salon and asked the young lady how much a haircut would cost. It was more than I wanted to pay, but I thought, "Well, I'd rather get it done now than take the time to run around."

I asked her, "How soon can you get me in?" She said, "We can take you right now. What's your name?" I told her and in a few minutes she began to take care of me. She used my name repeatedly, asking me questions about where I worked, what kind of work I did, if I was from Yakima, why I was in town, etc. She made great conversation, was warm, friendly and enthusiastic, and when she was all through she said, "Have a great weekend, Mr. Dennis."

She made me feel important because she continued to use my name. I love to hear my name, don't you? Each time we hear our name our mind short circuits in a positive way. So use your customers' names.

I met a client and his staff in the lounge of a resort on a weekend night. I had been sitting there for 30 to 45 seconds when the waiter approached, and asked, "Larry, what can I get you tonight?" My client responded with an astonished, "Boy, everyone knows you, don't they?" My response was to feel pretty important. The waiter, Phil, had heard my client greet me, "Hi, Larry," when I walked into the lounge. The waiter's alertness, awareness, and understanding of the importance of using a customer's name made a favorable hit. Since it was my first time to visit this resort, it made a favorable first impression on me.

My friend, Gordon Caudle, who manages a chain of hotels, knows how important it is to use the new guests' names when they are registering. After conducting a training class where he emphasized using the guests' names, Gordon was standing near a Russian-Chinese desk clerk who was hesitant about using guests' names. She handed an incoming guest, a Greek, a registration form, which he filled out. She took the registration form and, poor lady, the man's name was Stefano Andrepopoulus. She turned to Gordon and said, "Mr. Caudle, I'm sorry but I just can't pronounce his last name." At least she was trying, and this is what we all must do.

"Have To" or "Glad To"

Never say, "I'll **have to** look," "I'll **have to** order it for you," or "I'll **have to** ask my manager." That sounds like we are being put out by our customer. The correct response—and it isn't that different—is, "I'll be **glad to** look," "I'll be **glad to** check," or "Let me ask my manager. It will only take a second."

Phone Power

You may not speak on the phone with customers often. But the times you do are important. Here are some tips that can go a long way toward making you a phone professional.

Don't Say:

"If you don't send in your stub, we won't know where to apply the payment."

"Wait a minute."

"Hold the line."

"Hold on."

(After keeping someone waiting on the line) "That went out ____."

"The price will be ____."

"You have to ____."

"You must ____."

"Tell Mr. Smith to call Mr. Brown."

"You'll have to pay."

"You will be charged."

"You pay ____."

"Bye, bye."

"All-righty."

Suggested Phrases:

"By sending in the stub we can apply your payment properly."

"Do you mind waiting while I check that for you?"

"Would you like to wait, or may I call you back?"

"Thank you for waiting, Mrs. Black. I have the information for you."

"Would it be convenient for you ___?"

"It would clarify this if we could go over the receipts with you."

"Could you bring them along with you the next time you call at our office?"

"We would like to have _____."

"Would you have Mr. Smith call Bob Brown when he returns."

"Our records show a balance of ___."

"Service charge is ___."

"There is a charge for _____."

"Good-bye."

"All right."

Don't Say:

"Yah."

"Who's this?"

"Who's calling?"

"Could you call back?"

"What's your name?"

"What's the address?"

"What's your telephone number?"

"What information do you want?"

"You will have to call our Credit Department."

"You will have to talk to Mr. Brown."

"I don't know anything about that."

"I don't know what you're talking about."

"Speak up please."

"We can't do that for you until tomorrow."

"You didn't talk to me. I didn't take your call."

Suggested Phrases:

"Thank you for calling."

"May I tell him who's calling?" or "May I ask who is calling?"

"May I have him call you?"

"I'm sorry but I didn't get your name."

"May I have your name, please?"

"May I have your street address, Mr. Jones?"

"May I have your telephone number, Mr. Smith?"

"May I help you?"

"That information is in our Credit Department. May I transfer you?"

"Mr. Brown is familiar with that. May I transfer your call to him?"

"I'm sorry that information is not in this department. Could I locate the...?"

"Would you repeat that, please? I'm not sure I understood you, Mr. Jones."

"I'm sorry, I cannot hear you. Could you speak a little louder, please?"

"We'll be glad to take care of that for you. Could we schedule it for tomorrow?"

"I'm sorry, Mrs. Smith, I will be glad to take care of that for you."

Ben Franklin once said, "If you argue and contradict, you may achieve a victory sometimes; but it will be an empty victory because you will never get your opponent's good will."

Smart Alec In The Produce Department

Yesterday my wife and I were in the produce department of a local grocery store. I went over to look for baking potatoes and asked the young man who was there busily stocking produce, "Where are your baking potatoes?" He looked at me and said, "Right in front of you." It wasn't what he said but how he said it—his tone of voice—that I found objectionable. It was as if he had said, "Dummy, are you blind? Do you need a seeing-eye dog?" Do you think I will shop in that store a second time?

Later we returned to the produce department to look for some bananas and I saw two ladies—one sat in a wheelchair. The two women shoppers were looking for different items, filling up their shopping cart. The one helping the lady in the wheelchair said to the same young man, "Where are your turnip tops?" He said, "We don't have any turnip tops. We don't sell tops off turnips."

She replied, "Well, we've gotten tops here before." He said, "You expect me to cut the tops off turnips, then we'd have turnips without tops. We don't sell turnip tops." He didn't say, "I'm sorry," or "I wish we could..." T h e ladies picked up other greens and they went on their way. She was more understanding and patient than I would have been.

As we were checking out our purchases, the checker noticed that one of our yellow apples had a brown spot near the core. He said, "You don't want this one, do you?" I said, "Thanks for noticing." He took it out of the bag and threw it in the waste basket. I commented, "That's great customer service." He was really paying attention to his job, looking out for the best interest of the customer.

To Buy Or Not to Buy a Bike

This story was told to me by a friend who owns a bike shop:

"A man and woman came into our eastside store and he asked questions in her behalf about a bicycle. He kept on talking and the woman remained silent and stared at the floor. It was only after I got the woman by herself that she began to ask questions and was encouraged to take test rides. When it became apparent that she wanted a different bike than we carried, I suggested another store.

"She returned the following day having narrowed her selection to a bike from the other store and one I had shown her. Later that day she called and informed me she had chosen the other bike. I thanked her for shopping with us and suggested she could stop in any time with questions she might have and could buy her accessories from us.

"Our confidence in her ability to make her own decision, to raise her eyes from the floor, resulted in a customer who buys her bike accessories from us, and a friend who speaks well of us to other people.

"That's what the retail business is all about. She has become a commercial for us."

Take Home

By practicing your pleasant personality at work, you'll find that it rubs off on your family life. It's amazing that so many persons show the least amount of common courtesy and consideration for their own family members.

People who wouldn't think of speaking sharply to a supervisor or customer or friend may think nothing of barking at their wives or husbands. Courtesy is just as important to a happy home life as it is to a successful career.

My wife and I have been married 30 years. I'm not sure when it started, but when I ask Donna Lee if she could give me a cup of tea or hand something to me or do something special for me, her response is "Sure," in a warm, friendly, caring voice. Being courteous—smiling, saying, "Sure, I'll be glad to," can make a great difference in our family life.

Even though robots have no learning curve and machines don't go on strike, and even though the best managed businesses were heavily influenced by exotic electronic and computer-based office machinery, in the 1980's, we came to realize that the most important single person in an organization is the individual—the person who provides the sales and service.

Never make critical remarks about another employee or other department to customers. You can't sink the officers' quarters of a ship. If one department (i.e. shipping, repair service) goes down, we all go down. Never make critical comments, lose your temper, or display anger to other employees in front of customers. And keep your troubles to yourself, your aches and pains, your little physical quirks. A fellow asked me the other day, "Have I ever told you about my operation?"

I replied with a cheerful, "No, and I want to thank you for that!"

Our clients are quite willing to pay for what they want. Although the specifics of our product or service are a factor, we've found that a much more important issue is simply that we care. Customers want attention, recognition, and empathy, and they're willing to pay for it. People will go right on preferring to do business with friends and with people who care.

Just For Today

For just one day, we can do anything we set our hearts on. So, for this day only let us resolve to be unafraid of life, unafraid of death, unafraid to be happy, and vow to enjoy the beauty around us and believe only the best of others.

Just for today, let us live this day only. Let's forget yesterday and tomorrow and not try to solve the whole problem of life in one fell swoop.

Lincoln said people are just about as happy as they make up their minds to be. He was so right! We must vow to adjust ourselves to what is —our family, our business, our opportunities. To try to make the world over to suit us is a big order. If we cannot have what we like, we can like what we have.

So, just for today, let us be agreeable, responsive, cheerful, and kind. Let us look our best, walk softly, praise people for what they do, and not criticize them for what they cannot do. When we find fault let's overlook it. Don't you feel thankful when you get a second chance? Remember that the next fellow would appreciate it, too.

Your personality is a reflection of who you are. If you stop and think about how important the projection of yourself to others is, you may pause and think twice about giving a sharp answer when a soft one will do, a frown when a smile may win you friends, show impatience when forbearance may convert a person into a repeat customer.

Chapter 5

– E –

Enthusiasm

"Nothing great was ever achieved without enthusiasm."

Ralph Waldo Emerson

Enthusiasm comes from the Greek **en-theos, en** meaning **inside, theos the root of the English word, theology.** To the Greeks it meant "God in us—Spirit indwelling." Enthusiasm seems to be a misunderstood term. We tend to confuse enthusiasm and animation. They are not the same. Enthusiasm is deep. It wells up from within, it is as abiding as love. Enthusiasm comes from the heart out, not from the teeth out. The truly enthusiastic person loves his job, his customers, and is excited about **what he does** and **why he does it.**

This attitude is reflected in Edgar Guests' lines of advice to the shop owner:

If I possessed a shop or store
I'd drive the grouches off my floor.
I'd never let some gloomy guy
Offend the folks who come to buy.
I'd never keep a boy or clerk
With mental toothache at his work,
Nor let a man who draws my pay
Drive customers of mine away.
I'd treat the man who takes my time
And spends a nickel or a dime;
With courtesy and make him feel
That I was pleased to close the deal,
Because tomorrow, who can tell,
He may want the stuff I have to sell;
And in that case then glad he'll be
To spend his dollars all with me.

The reason people pass one door
To patronize another store
Is not because the busier place
Has better silks or gloves or lace
Or cheaper prices, but it lies
In pleasant words and smiling eyes;
The only difference, I believe
Is in the treatment folks receive.

It is good business to be fair
To keep a bright and cheerful air
About the place; and not to show
Your customers how much you know.

Whatever any patron did
I'd try to keep my temper hid,
And never let him spread along

The word that I had done him wrong.

Edgar A. Guest

Synonyms for enthusiasm include ardor, eagerness, excitement, fervor, optimism, fire, and force. There are no enthusiastic pessimists, enthusiastic cynics, or enthusiastic critics. Passion—thanks to Tom Peters and his best-selling book *A Passion for Excellence*—is a word we have rediscovered. Enthusiastic people have a passion for their work and for their lives. That doesn't mean they enjoy every detail; it doesn't mean that their work is free from routine and drudgery. It means they have learned to see beyond the commonplace by concentrating on the things they like about their job and the opportunities their job affords them.

A passerby curiously watched a construction crew. "What are you doing?" he asked the superintendent.

"Putting up a wall," he retorted, "what does it look like I am doing?" A few minutes later he put the same question to a laborer who was pushing a wheelbarrow.

"Building a cathedral to the glory of God!" he responded and on he passed.

There seemed to be a glow in his demeanor, a lightness in his step. It is our belief in the importance of what we do that can turn drudgery and routine monotony into joy.

Thermostat vs. Thermometer

In the summer of 1974, I had the privilege of training Raymond Berry and his wife, Sally, in an exciting five-week personal development course in Oak Park, Michigan. Raymond Berry, as you may know, was known as an outstanding receiver when he played for the Baltimore

Colts and was inducted into the Pro Football Hall of Fame in 1973. At the time Raymond participated in my training program, he was the backfield coach for the Detroit Lions. He has subsequently become head coach for the New England Patriots. During his second season with the Patriots, Raymond took the team to the Super Bowl.

When Raymond finished our program he said, "Larry, your program has helped me be more like a thermostat and less like a thermometer." As you know, thermometers register the atmosphere around them; if they are good they will give you an accurate readout. Thermostats control the atmosphere. There are two kinds of people: thermometers—those who register the atmosphere, and thermostats—those rare people who control what's going on inside their head and hearts, regardless of what their outer circumstances may be.

Real enthusiasm is when, regardless of the outer circumstances, we somehow develop our ability to control our response, we develop a sort of emotional reserve, a fundamental context for our life which colors all of the events of our lives with a positive shading. Regardless of the customer's complaint or the pressures of the day or the shortages that occur, we have that rare but important ability to remain in control of our emotions and project an optimistic, positive feeling to those around us.

Enthusiasm is contagious.

Years ago I was the keynote speaker for the annual sales meeting of Hardware Wholesale Inc. (HWI) in Ft. Wayne, Indiana. Their sales representatives call on retail hardware stores throughout the Midwest. At one point during the presentation I said, "Thermometers are a dime a dozen." One of the salesmen in the audience spoke up and said, "No they're not. They're 79 cents a piece."

The point is: a thermometer has significantly less

value than a thermostat. Mechanical thermostats are so common we take them for granted. Can you imagine what it would be like to have to turn your heat up every time you are cool in the winter, or turn it down every time you are too warm? I remember those cold mornings in Michigan when I was a boy. We'd stoke up the old furnace. In a little while it was so hot it would drive us out. Then we would shut off the dampers, and not too much later, it was so cold that we opened the dampers once again. Then we stood over the heat register waiting for the heat to come up again.

Today a quality thermostat controls the temperature to within a four-degree variance. Most of us even take for granted the automatic thermostats in our cars. In our modern world, we do take mechanical thermostats for granted. Yet the people who are thermostats—who have that rare ability to control what is happening inside their hearts and heads, who remain cool and collected under stressful circumstances and optimistic and positive under negative circumstances—are so rare that they are never taken for granted. They are always sought after.

Enthusiasm is that quality which enables us to insulate ourselves from negative influences and circumstances. Enthusiasm enables us to impact and literally determine our circumstances. When you are enthusiastic it rubs off on others. People are influenced by your optimistic approach to problem-solving, challenges, and difficulties. Enthusiasm is like the measles, and no one is immune.

When we first think of enthusiasm, it seems like some have it and some don't. We all know people who express a certain joy about living and others who cringe at the outset of another day—Andy Capp with his black cloud, Chicken Little crying out, "The sky is falling!"—and those people who invite us to their "pity parties" on a daily basis. In our desire to label and explain things we may oversimplify. We are all enthusiastic about something at one time or another. We all lack enthusiasm sometimes, too. What is the distinguishing factor?

We define enthusiasm as <u>commitment</u> in <u>action</u>. Let's see what great people have said about enthusiasm:

George Washington Carver: "Anything will give up its secret if you love it enough."

Coleman Cox: "When enthusiasm is inspired by reason, is practical in application, reflects confidence and spreads good cheer, raises morale, inspires associates, arouses loyalty, and laughs at adversity, it is beyond price."

Michael de Montaigne: "The most evident token and apparent sign of true wisdom is a constant and unconstrained rejoicing."

Charles Schwab: "A person can succeed at almost anything he has unlimited enthusiasm for."

Lord Byron: "On with the dance! Let joy be unconfined."

At first glance it may seem that people who have things "going their way" are enthusiastic. The ones who draw a tougher lot in life aren't enthusiastic. This seems to indicate that when a person has the right amount of money, enough good friends, or great weather during a vacation, then they are enthusiastic. However, we all know people who don't match these stereotypes. If we look honestly at ourselves, we can remember times when even the bluest skies or any amount of money could not awaken us out of our depression. And on the other hand, we've experienced times when even the darkest storm couldn't dampen our enthusiasm. It seems safe to say that enthusiasm is not a result of life's circumstances.

If enthusiasm does not depend upon what is occurring in our lives, then we may be wise to look inside ourselves for its source. Sometimes we express enthusiasm and sometimes we don't. The truth is, we have a choice in the matter. We can't control what happens in our world, but we can choose how we react to what shows up in our lives. When challenged by life we can respond with enthusiasm or resignation. We believe that an enthusiastic attitude has a great deal to do with what we accomplish and how successful we become. Calvin Coolidge said that the determination to succeed in an endeavor is more fundamental to the outcome than other factors such as education and intelligence. Enthusiasm and determination are the muscles of accomplishment. They can be exercised at any time. The circumstances in our lives are the result of the enthusiasm or zest we have for life.

Sappers

Take a look at the people you enjoy being around. Not many folks hang around a depressed, despondent person. Psychologists even have a name for negative people—they call them "sappers." Sappers are surrounded by a negative force field. You can feel it when you walk into their department or business. Your best insulation is to stay away from them. People who are happy and interested in life are more fun to be with than negative people and chronic complainers. Everybody loves to be around enthusiastic people, with the possible exception of committed pessimists.

Work is seldom the thing that tires. Our attitude toward our work determines how we feel at the end of the day. By being enthusiastic and courteous on the job you will go home feeling better. Boredom, resentfulness, and irritability make our jobs hard. Enthusiasm and courtesy make our jobs easier and our customers come back. A happy nature generates calmness of spirit and eliminates nervous fatigue and tension.

Courtesy is fun, it helps renew our energy, it helps maintain our enthusiasm. Being courteous and considerate produces a quality that feeds on itself. The enthusiastic person is courteous and considerate, the considerate and courteous person is enthusiastic. It's truly a win-win situation.

The active participation method we use in our programs sometimes causes participants to conclude that we are confused about the difference between enthusiasm and animation. We realize the difference. Animation comes from the teeth out. Animation is a sign of life, but we've all known people who come on too strong. They are unbelievable. Enthusiasm comes from the heart out. Enthusiasm is deep and abiding, as love is deep and abiding. Enthusiasm is that special essence, that potentially divine spark that separates the powerful, winning person from the dull, drab, dead drudges who drag through life.

A Moving Experience

A great friend of mine was transferred across the country by his company. He sold his house, bought another, and moved his family. Please remember that a new job, a new house, and a move are all on the list of the top ten causes of stress. He'd only been in his new job for about a month when his manager called him in and said, "I want you to be more professional. You're too enthusiastic."

How can anyone be too enthusiastic? Is it possible to be too committed to excellence? Is it possible to be too optimistic, too determined to find a better way, too eager to make projects work? And since when are professionalism and enthusiasm in conflict? When this friend came to me and told me his story, he was scared, depressed, and confused. He said, "What do you think I should do?' We talked about it, and I gave him the best advice I could. The good news is a few weeks later his boss was relieved of his responsibility and my friend has subsequently received a significant promotion.

I've discovered that for many people their enthusiasm is the best-kept secret in town. I remember Russell Brownbush telling about the time he was given a project by his manager at the phone company. He called his team members to his office and explained all the details of the project in a flat, drab, intellectual way. After they left the office, he stood up behind his desk, beat his hand in his palm, and said, "Wow, this is going to be great! Wow, this is going to be exciting! Wow, I can't wait to tackle this!" Yet he had talked about this project to his team in such a passive, uninspiring, unanimated way. I say, "If anything, let's go to the other extreme." Most of us have room for a little animation, most of us have room to let a little carnival barker out.

Our daughter-in-law, Juliana Dennis, was the youngest manager in the history of a prominent retail clothing specialty store chain. She was recently promoted to the Walnut Creek branch, the fourth largest in the company's chain. At age twenty-seven she manages more than a thousand employees in a store that will do over one hundred million dollars in volume this year. Before she received the promotion at a store managers' meeting in Seattle, Washington, another store manager asked her, "Are you on something?" Isn't it amazing that some people think you have to rely on outside stimulants to be up, enthusiastic, and excited about life.

Julianna is excited about her job, her life, and her opportunities with her company. She is excited about the challenges she faces in her job and she celebrates each of her successes as she meets those challenges with success.

How do you generate more enthusiasm for life? It's simple: cultivate the ability to love living. Love people, love the sky under which you live, love beauty. The person who loves becomes enthusiastic, filled with the sparkle and the joy of life. If you're not enthusiastic, begin today to cultivate the love of living. Thomas Edison once said, "When a man dies, if he can pass enthusiasm along to his children, he has left them an estate of incalculable value." Ralph Waldo Emerson wrote, "Every great and commanding moment in the annals of the world is the triumph of some enthusiasm."

Frank Bettger's book, *How I Raised Myself from Failure to Success in Selling,* was a great source of inspiration to thousands, and when I heard his speech on a training film I was inspired. But when I saw Frank live, at eighty-two years old, standing before an audience with his red suspenders, full of life, fire, zest, and force, I was amazed. He challenged the audience to take the pledge to be five times more enthusiastic about an important and challenging area in their lives. I was impressed that enthusiasm had to go beyond an idea, beyond a concept. Enthusiasm had to become, for me and others, a commitment to step away from normality and attack an area of life with this renewing force as if it were impossible to fail.

I began to challenge my classes to take the pledge, to be five times more enthusiastic about an important and challenging area of their lives. I immediately saw greater results in our classes, I now make this challenge to you, the same one Frank Bettger made to me. Pick an area of your life in which you have experienced less than satisfactory results, an area in which you have been "talking a good game," an area in which you have been procrastinating. Take the pledge: be five times more enthusiastic and watch out for the exciting results.

In 1985, when Russ Schildan was challenged to apply five times more enthusiasm to an area of his life in which he had lacked commitment, he thought of his '55 Studebaker Commander, a speedster model. He and his wife had begun restoring it in 1966. After working on the car for about four years, they put it in storage for the winter in Salem, Oregon, at $50 a month. It stayed there for ten years. That begins to add up. Russ decided to change his commitment, to redouble his efforts, and in *four weeks* the car was running. When I talked with Russ in July of 1989, he began to enthusiastically share the unique features of his Studebaker. I could tell that he and his wife enjoy driving it on a daily basis. Enthusiasm makes the difference. And sustained enthusiasm brings long-term joy and fulfillment into our lives.

Johnny Johnson had engineered the idea of using a 455 cubic-inch Oldsmobile Toronado engine in a Sandrail. To his knowledge, this hadn't been done before. Most Sandrails have VW engines and some have Pinto power. After Johnny bought a Toronado, he said his commitment was sort of half-hearted and doubts began to plague him. The car had been sitting under a tree in his back yard for 18 months. We challenged Johnny to give his project five times more enthusiasm. He redoubled his commitment, becoming far more enthusiastic. In four weeks he had not only completed the Sandrail, but had built a similar one with his neighbor. He used up 180 pounds of welding rod in the process. When I talked with Johnny three years later, he told me, "It's still running the fastest Sandrail at Sand Lake. Come on out and we'll have some fun." When we apply five times more enthusiasm to our lives we can come out of ourselves and we have a lot more fun.

The Boiling Point

Water at 211 degrees has little value. You can't do much with water at that temperature except perhaps scald yourself. But by adding one degree to that temperature you raise it to 212 degrees and it converts to steam. With steam, properly harnessed, you can literally move mountains. Most people are living their lives at something less than 212 degrees. Their lives are a lot like 7-Up that has been left in the refrigerator with the cap off for a week. It has all the ingredients, the sugar, the calories, the flavoring, but one thing is missing: the carbonation. People without enthusiasm are like flat 7-Up. They have lost that zest, that bubble. Enthusiasm gives our lives zest and bubble.

Hot Spot

My wife, Donna Lee, and I were recently driving through Central Oregon. It was about two in the afternoon and we were getting hungry. I had seen a Mexican restaurant in the town we had just driven through, so we turned around, drove back, and pulled up in front of the restaurant. It didn't look very appealing from the outside. There was a young man standing in front of the door. I asked him, "Is this a good place to eat?"

He replied, "It sure is," as he walked over and stuck his head in our front window.

I said, "Are you sure about that?"

His response was, "Absolutely. This is the best Mexican restaurant in town! Come on in and you'll be glad you did."

I asked, "Can we park here?"

He said, "Of course."

We went inside. It turned out that he was our waiter. We enjoyed the meal, but most of all we enjoyed his enthusiastic service. We probably wouldn't have gone in at all if he hadn't been convincing in his response to our questions. He wasn't tentative, he didn't say, "I don't know how you'll like it, it depends on how hot you like Mexican food, depends on your taste" or any other qualifying comments. He was emphatic in his enthusiasm for his restaurant.

How about you? Are you willing to take a stand, make a commitment? This is an important part of real enthusiasm.

Selling Chryslers

Walter P. Chrysler was once asked, "What do you look for in an employee?" He said, "I look for skill, ability, knowledge and technique, experience, background and training. But far more important than background and technical expertise, I look for people who are enthusiastic about Chrysler. When they're enthusiastic about Chrysler, they get others enthusiastic about Chrysler who get others enthusiastic about Chrysler. And as a result we build better Chryslers and we sell more, too."

Somewhere along the way Chrysler may have lost this

philosophy, but Lee Iacocca brought enthusiasm back, and like the mythical Phoenix Bird, Chrysler rose from the ashes of defeat. Enthusiasm will do the same for you! No matter how far down you may have fallen or how defeated you may feel, enthusiasm will turn the tide, will carry the day.

Shakespeare said, "Assume a virtue though you have it not." You may be thinking now, "What if I don't feel enthusiastic?" Assume the virtue. **Act** enthusiastic. And that's what William James, professor at Harvard and father of American psychology, said years later. He said, "The greatest discovery of my generation is that people can change their lives by changing their mental attitude." But how do you change your attitude? William James gave us the secret to that, too. He said you can't always control your attitude but you can always control your actions. And if you will act a certain way you will feel that way. The feeling follows the action. In other words, **act** enthusiastic and you'll **be** enthusiastic. Act friendly and you will be friendly. Which comes first, feeling happy or smiling? Smiling or feeling happy? Try it and you will discover that you immediately feel better, happier when you smile.

—1776—

Paul Hamlin, my wife, Donna Lee, and I were sitting in the New Theatre in London, England, watching the play "1776." I saw Paul take a three-by-five card out of his pocket (he always had a three-by-five card in his pocket) and make a note. When we left the theatre, I said, "I bet I know exactly what you wrote on that card." And I was right. What he had written were the lines spoken in the play when the stage lights dimmed and a spotlight was directed to John Adams. John Adams had been stuck in

Philadelphia for a year, and had seen his beloved wife Abigail in Virginia only on rare occasions. The Constitutional Convention had been dragging on and John Adams, who was instrumental in holding the Convention together, was discouraged and depressed when he wrote these words:

"Dear Abigail, am I a visionary? Am I imprudent? Am I impractical? Do I dream dreams that can never be? I'm tired and I want to come home."

In the play we saw the stage turn black and then Abigail appeared in the spotlight on the other side of the stage. She replied to her husband, "Dear John, you are not impractical, you are not imprudent, you do not dream dreams that will never be. It was you who taught me there are only two kinds of men of value, those who make commitments and those who challenge others to commitment. Stay there."

This is the seemingly secret element of real enthusiasm. Commitment—unswerving, unreserved commitment.

Ralph Waldo Emerson wrote, "Every great and commanding moment in the annals of the world is the triumph of some enthusiasm." Renew your enthusiasm for your opportunities, for your work, for your life. In doing so, declare your independence from mediocrity and complacency."

Take a few moments to choose a project that will benefit from your "renewed commitment"—your five times more enthusiasm. Write down that project and the steps you will take to renew your commitment and achieve your goal.

Here are six major areas for you to consider:

Physical: Do you want to change your eating habits? Start an exercise plan? A diet?

Financial: Would you like to pay off a loan? Develop an investment plan? Save more money?

Mental: Do you want to take a class? Learn a language? Is there an unfinished book you want to read?

Social: Do you want to become more involved in community service? Do volunteer work? Invite your friends over for dinner more often?

Family: Would you like to spend more quality time with your family? Improve your relationship with your parents, children, wife or husband?

Spiritual: Is there room for renewal to your spiritual community? Would you like to improve your spiritual life?

Take a moment to fill in the blank space below. This exercise is the final step towards more enthusiasm in your life:

What is the project, the *area* of your life, to which you are willing to pledge five times as much enthusiasm as you are now generating?_____

_____

What result do you want to achieve?_____

_____

What steps will you take to redouble your enthusiasm for this project?_____

_____

How will you know when you have caused the turn-around?_____

_____

What is your pay-off for making the commitment to achieve five times more enthusiasm and sticking with it ?

_____

_____

As a result of teaching classes over the past twenty-five years, I have had many, many class members approach me at breaks, before and after giving talks, and ask, "Are you this way all the time? Are you this enthusiastic all the time?" Since my wife has worked with me in many of my classes, people will often approach her and ask the same question. Of course I'm tired at the end of a long day or a long week. She's seen me fall asleep on the couch more than once.

Being tired after long hours of work is normal. I have my down days just like anyone else. What may be different about me, and apparently is, is that I have the ability to live my life full-out when it's time to play the game. My sons have confirmed to their friends and my wife has confirmed to our class members and others that I am positive, optimistic, and excited 99 percent of the time.

Frank Bettger in his book, *How I Raised Myself from Failure to Success in Selling,* chronicles his experience with the life-changing power of enthusiasm:

Shortly after I started out as a professional baseball player, I got one of the biggest shocks of my life. That was back in 1907. I was playing for Johnstown, Pennsylvania in the tri-State League. I was young and ambitious— wanted to get to the top—and what happened? I was fired! My whole life might have been different if I hadn't gone to the manager and asked him why he fired me. In fact, I wouldn't have the real privilege of writing this book if I hadn't asked him that question.

The manager said he fired me because I was lazy! Well, that was the last thing I expected him to say.

"You drag yourself around the field like a veteran who has been playing ball for twenty years," he told me. "Why do you act that way if you're not lazy?"

"Well, Bert," I said, "I'm so nervous, so scared, that I want to hide my fear from the crowd, and especially from the other players on the team. Besides, I hope that by taking it easy, I'll get rid of my nervousness."

"Frank," he said, "it will never work. That's the thing that is holding you down. Whatever you do after you leave here, for heaven's sake, wake yourself up, and put some life and enthusiasm into your work!" I had been making $175 a month at Johnstown. After being fired there, I went down to Chester, Pennsylvania in the Atlantic League where they paid me only $25 a month. Well, I couldn't feel very enthusiastic on that kind of money, but I began to act enthusiastic. After I was there three days, an old ball player, Danny Meehan, came to me and said: "Frank, what in the world are you doing down here in a rank bush-league like this?"

"Well, Danny," I replied, "if I knew how to get a better job, I'd go anywhere."

A week later, Danny induced New Haven, Connecticut to give me a trial. My first day in New Haven will always stand out in my memory as a great event in my life. No one knew me in that league, so I made a resolution that nobody would ever accuse me of being lazy. I made up my mind to establish the reputation of being the most enthusiastic ball player they'd ever seen in the New England League. I thought if I could establish such a reputation, than I'd have to live up to it.

From the minute I appeared on the field, I acted like a man electrified. I acted as though I were alive with a million batteries. I threw the ball around the diamond so fast and so hard that it almost knocked our infielder's hands apart. Once, apparently trapped, I slid into third base with so much energy and force that the third baseman fumbled the ball and I was able to score an important run. Yes, it was all a show, an act I was putting on. The thermometer that day was nearly 100 degrees. I wouldn't have been surprised if I had dropped over with a sunstroke the way I ran around the field.

Did it work? It worked like magic. Three things happened:

1. My enthusiasm almost entirely overcame my fear. In fact, my nervousness began to work for me, and I played far better than I ever thought I was capable of playing. (If you are nervous be thankful. Don't hold it back. Turn it on. Let your nerves work for you.)

2. My enthusiasm affected the other players on the team, and they, too, became enthusiastic.

3. Instead of dropping with the heat, I felt better during the game and after it was over than I had ever felt before.

My biggest thrill came the following morning when I read in the New Haven newspaper: "This new player, Bettger, was a barrel of enthusiasm. He inspired our boys. They not only won the game, but looked better than at any time this season."

The newspapers began calling me "Pep" Bettger—the life of the team. I mailed the newspaper clippings to Bert Conn, manager of Johnstown. Can you imagine the expression on his face as he read about "Pep" Bettger, the dud he'd tied a can to three weeks before—for being **lazy**?

Within ten days, **enthusiasm** took me from $25 a month to $185 a month—it increased my income by 700 percent. Let me repeat—nothing but the determination to act enthusiastic increased my income 700 percent in ten days. I got this stupendous increase in salary not because I could throw a ball better—or catch or hit better, not because I had any more ability as a ball player. I didn't know any more about baseball than I did before.

Action stimulates energy. People who go into action have more energy. If you wait to feel like doing it, you may never do it. If you do it, you'll feel like it. Secondly, action stimulates confidence. If, when you are a customer, you see a salesperson take decisive action, it builds your confidence in that person. And if you act confident, even though you don't feel it, you'll be confident.

You, too, can literally change your life and influence the lives of everyone one you meet...with enthusiasm. Start today, it will really pay.

Chapter 6

– A –

Action

"...The test of any man lies in action."

Pindar

Promptness is the first sign of reliability. Move! Move! Move! Do something even if it is wrong. Remember, actions do speak louder than words. The lack of animation shown by those who are in business to **serve** the customer continually annoys me. The biggest consumer complaint is waiting. What we want is **action.**

Action is important for two reasons. First, action stimulates energy. People who act have more energy. If you wait to feel like doing something, you may never do it. Second, action stimulates confidence. Seeing a salesperson take decisive action builds your confidence in that person. If you lack confidence yourself, action will help you be confident.

Have you ever had the experience of feeling like you were an interruption to what the salesperson was doing before you came in, like stocking shelves was more important that greeting you?

Greeting the customer is a most important action. The legendary Sam Walton of Wal-Mart considers this so important that he hires official "greeters" for his stores. The Marriott Hotels, through computer hookup, can tell if you have ever stayed in a Marriott. If you have, after you have given them your name and they have looked up your reservation they say "Welcome back, Mr. ___!" Last night my wife and I went out to a video store. The clerk behind the counter was busy talking on the phone, too busy to acknowledge us. We were annoyed and impatient, so we left. That video store didn't get my first-time business or my repeat business.

Eugene H. Fram, a marketing professor at the Rochester Institute of Technology, believes that in the future, businesses will guarantee the customer's time, as well as the product. The rise in the number of dual-earner families has put consumers' time at a premium, therefore, many people will be willing to pay for a guarantee that ensures service scheduling at the customer's convenience or compensates customers for time lost during product servicing.

Don't Just Stand There...

Not long ago I visited a privately owned used car lot in Tigard, Oregon. I'd been thinking about purchasing a pickup truck for our family and business use. The salesroom was staffed with one person—the owner, apparently. He was talking on the phone with what sounded like another dealer. He talked and talked, never acknowledging or recognizing me. After a few minutes I left. I haven't been back. I love the pickup I bought from his competitor.

We recently spent the weekend at Sunriver, Oregon,

one of the Northwest's most exclusive resorts. While we were there, we visited many shops as we always like to do. My wife went into a high-fashion shop while I visited with a friend at Sunriver Realty.

When Donna Lee came out she said, "I was in there five minutes and no one ever said a word to me. Two of the salespeople walked right by me, visiting with each other, but they never said a word to me."

Sometimes salespeople think they're being polite by not "bugging" their customers. Donna Lee didn't take it that way. A greeting is always appropriate: "Are you enjoying the beautiful weather this weekend?" "Do you get to come over often?"

Speed — Now!

The walk-in medical clinic is a response to the expectations and demands for immediate attention. The eyeglasses-in-an-hour clinic is an example of how the desire for immediate attention and action, combined with modern technology, has resulted in a whole new approach to servicing the glasses needs of the customer. The while-you-wait film processors are another example of our demand for immediate action. The fast food industry is more dated but still an example of our demand for immediate action. We want action and we want it now.

Not long ago Skipper's, a Northwest fish franchise, ran TV commercials which said, "We promise that if you don't have your lunch within eleven minutes, we'll give it to you free." Their commercials were extremely successful, and now Denny's Family Restaurants are advertising, "If you don't have your meal within 10 minutes of ordering, it will be free." And Domino's Pizza: "We deliver in 30 minutes or your pizza free." The focus isn't on quality, price, comfort, or location. The focus is on speed, action, and immediate attention.

What about you? What are you doing in your business to give your customers immediate action and attention? Are you playing hard-to-get? Are you playing it cool? Are you trying to act professional by putting your customers in a line and keeping them waiting? Time is money. Yesterday I read a headline that said a contractor on a bridge project will be fined $41.18 *per minute* if the project isn't completed by the deadline.

Our customers may not be able to fine us $41.18 per minute, but they will fine us by not doing repeat business with us. We at Turbo Management Systems challenge and promise our clients to help them achieve significant strides toward being world-class companies. We define "world class" as the highest possible quality at the lowest effective cost with the *quickest customer response time*. Who do you ask to wait? *Fully a third of what is required to be "world class" is fast service.* Where can you speed up your customer response?

Pro-Active Versus Passive

Over the Christmas holidays we visited our sons in the San Francisco Bay area. Our 21-year-old, Loren Dennis, had recently begun selling shoes at Nordstrom's downtown San Francisco store. My wife and I had heard so many great things about this fantastic store that we were eager to see it and, of course, to view our son in action. Loren had sold more shoes the previous day than anyone else in the store, over $2,000 worth. I was curious to see why. I learned and unlearned a great deal as I watched my son in action.

What stood out immediately, as I observed his

behavior, was the fact that he was always in command of the sale situation. He presented customers not only with the shoes they thought they wanted, but other models that might please them. The result was not a decision on the customer's part to buy a pair of shoes, but which of those offered to choose. He was being what I call an active salesman.

Normally when we consider customer response we usually think in a reactive mode—responding to the customer when he approaches the counter. But the pro-active salesperson anticipates his customers' needs. The ultimate in response to the customer is demonstrated when the salesperson anticipates the customer's needs before he expresses them. The automatic refill in my home-heating oil tank is a great example. Our oil dealer is a pro-active salesperson. He knows I need oil before I do through a carefully designed system which tracks outside temperatures and coordinates them with the history of oil use in our house under similar weather conditions.

Here is an idea that is sure to increase your repeat business: Call 10 customers today who bought something yesterday or last week. Ask them, "How did we do?" and for goodness sakes, *listen*—really listen. When they have concluded their comments, *thank them*, take any appropriate action, and remember to write them a note expressing your gratitude for their interest and patronage of your company. (See Chapter 7.)

What are you doing to be pro-active? What are you doing to help your customer know what he needs before he wants it and provide it before he needs it?

The question I challenge you to honestly ask yourself is, "In what ways can I improve my response time? How can you improve your response time with your customers inside the company and your traditional customers outside?

How can you better anticipate their needs? How can *you* know what they want before *they* know what they want?" By improving your response time, you will solve the biggest consumer complaint of all: waiting.

Moment of Truth

A young man was overheard talking on the pay phone. "Hello, Mr. Blackwell, do you have someone to mow your lawn? You do. Does he do a good job? Does he trim around the edges when he is through? Does he clean up all the trimmings? Does he put the tools away when he is finished? Is he fairly priced? Well, okay then."

As he started to walk away, a businessman who had overheard the conversation said, "Sorry you didn't get the job."

"Oh," he said, "I already have the job. I was just checking up on myself."

How about calling your customers, identifying yourself and immediately thanking them for shopping at your store. Let them know you sincerely appreciate their business and ask them if they have just two minutes to answer a few questions about your level of service. Include questions such as, "Was the parking lot clear of baskets and were the floors and windows clean?" "Did we make eye contact and appear to be sincere about serving your every need?" "Did you get the help you needed in finding everything you wanted?"

Those who have taken this approach to customer service have found that over 35 percent of their customers have time for the survey and really don't mind the call. Actually, most seem to appreciate the attention.

Keep 'Em Smiling

Nothing makes Ron Einspahr more furious than hearing people bad-mouth car salesmen. Sure, he concedes, the industry has its share of unscrupulous operators. But for the hard-working owner of Einspahr Auto Plaza in Brookings, South Dakota, the importance of selling cars has taken a backseat to a different goal: superior customer service. Ron is less concerned with keeping track of sales and focuses instead on tallying his satisfied buyers.

Einspahr or one of his employees calls up every customer three days after the sale to find out if any problems have cropped up. He automatically follows up after 30 days, and again once every year, to check if his customers are still satisfied. When he finds a problem, he does "whatever it takes" to solve it.

Just What Does a Customer Want?

The other day a member of our office staff came in steaming mad. That morning when her husband opened a package of shirts just back from the laundry, he couldn't find one that could be worn. Collar buttons were missing, one was torn, and the others were sloppily pressed. On her way to the office, she stopped in at the laundry to bring the shirts back. Evidently, the man behind the counter wasn't fully awake since it was before nine o'clock. His answers left her madder than ever and also cost him a customer.

What does a customer want...whether it's from a laundry, an automobile dealership, or from your store:

1. The customer wants courtesy and a friendly attitude. He doesn't want to be treated as a stranger.

2. The customer wants honesty. If we don't know the

answer, say so rather than give a wrong one.

3. The customer wants complete and expert attention given to his problem. If the person serving him can't give him help, somebody else who can should be brought into the act.

4. The customer wants recognition and to know that we are interested in their welfare.

5. The customer wants what he wants promptly. If there has to be a delay, he wants to know why and for how long.

6. The customer wants satisfaction. And if we perform on the first five requirements we've listed, he will be satisfied.

To sum up... the customer wants to be treated as if he is the number one person in our universe...and when we are talking or dealing with them, he is.

On a scale of one to ten, to what degree are you looking for opportunities to give each customer more than he would get doing business with your competition? Do you believe that your primary responsibility is to behave with customers in a manner that causes them to brag enthusiastically to others about their experience?

The Customer

A CUSTOMER is the most important person in any business.

A CUSTOMER is not dependent on us—we are dependent on them.

A CUSTOMER is not an interruption of our work—he is

the reason for it.

A CUSTOMER does us a favor when he calls—we are not doing him a favor by serving him.

A CUSTOMER is a part of our business—not an outsider.

A CUSTOMER is not a cold statistic—he is a flesh-and-blood human being with feelings and emotions like our own.

A CUSTOMER is not someone to argue or match wits with.

A CUSTOMER is a person who brings us his wants—it is our job to fill those wants.

A CUSTOMER is deserving of the most courteous and attentive treatment we can give him.

A CUSTOMER is the life-blood of every business.

A customer is a person who buys goods or services from us. You, too, are a customer. From whom do you buy? Do you enjoy being treated as a special person? Do you get aggravated by people who fail to treat you courteously, who fail to value your importance as a customer to them? Of course, you do. But just remember you are providing someone else with a service or product. Do you think of how you would like to be treated when you deal with that someone else? If you always remember to change places mentally with the person you are serving, you'll treat him more fairly, and you will be developing a repeat customer.

Chapter 7

— T —

Thank You

"When you drink from the stream remember the spring."

Chinese Proverb

Thank you is more than two little words. These two words express an attitude of gratitude, a fundamental outlook on life that adds joy to all we experience. Saying "thank you" is our way of expressing our appreciation for the time and efforts of others.

Everybody wants to be appreciated. Being appreciated is a fundamental desire. Yet an attitude of gratitude is often replaced with an attitude of "attitude." An attitude of taking others for granted. An attitude of expecting a person to give us his business, his patronage. When taken to extremes, this attitude leads to cynicism, impatience, sloppiness, and inefficiencies, showing up in every area of our business. It results in our being less responsive and less concerned. Our products and services will be less attuned to our customers' needs. We will lose our competitive advantage. Saying **thank you** is so simple, yet we still don't do it enough. You can't over-thank your customer.

How we like to be thanked for the business we give to anyone. My dentist gives me a fresh-cut carnation when I leave his office. What a way to say "thank you."

Winning at the Race Track

One of our clients is the owner of a prominent Greyhound race track. On a typical Saturday the company receives more than three thousand customers. Management asked us to work with their staff to improve customer courtesy, in every department, which included parking lot attendants, gate-persons, waiters, waitresses, ushers and parimutuel tellers. We endeavored to train every person who came in contact with the guests.

We developed a theme: "**WIN**." The **W** stands for Welcome. Our intention was to help everybody who had any contact with guests to welcome them quickly. The **I** stands for Involvement. What we meant by this was to nod, smile, say hello, ask a question. The **N** stands for Now. Take action immediately. *Do it Now!*

The results at the end of one year were significant improvements in customer feedback, notes, and comments. At the end of two years, we saw a remarkable increase in "handle" (amount wagered) to record highs.

One of the most important things we did was encourage *every* guest contact person to say "Thank you" when the guest was leaving his area or leaving the facility. So, as the guests left the restaurant we trained the waiters, waitresses, and buspersons to say, "Thank you," "Good Night," "See you next week." We trained the gate-people to make the same salutation, the very simple "Thank you" and "Good night." We trained every teller to say "Thank you." We trained everyone to say "Thank You." The last thing guests saw and heard was someone giving them the salutation, "Thank you."

You'd think it would be pretty tiring as people are pulling out of the parking lot by the hundreds to say to each person as they're leaving, "Thank you." Yet the results, as I've already indicated, have been significant. And the truth is, having an appreciative attitude isn't tiring at all. Instead it's energizing, invigorating, and enriching.

We can say "Thank you" in many ways. This past Friday I attended an open forum meeting. The moderator of the forum, Murray McBride, recently gave me a lead that has turned into a nice consulting contract for our firm. I had said "Thanks" once or twice. I wrote him a short note. This past Friday I passed him a check for $50.00. **One day** later, I had a note in the mail from Murray saying "Thanks, I will love to give you more leads."

You don't have to write a check to let people know you appreciate their business. A great way to say "Thanks" is to write thank-you notes. If you take the time to write three notes a day you will be light years ahead of your competitors. You will secure the loyalty of your customers. You will secure *repeat business*.

Here are some ideas for *Thank-you notes:*

I'm a better person for having met you.

Thank you for your confidence in me. It was my pleasure to be of service to you.

It is my business to see that you continue to be satisfied. Please do not hesitate to call whenever I can be of further service to you.

You can be assured that (name your company) and I will do everything possible to...

It was my pleasure meeting you and having the opportunity to introduce you to...(name of product)

Nothing excites me more than helping someone grow more successful.

I am very happy for you. I know you will have no problem getting (describe benefits of your products).

Please give me a call if any questions arise.

It's been my pleasure helping you get easily on your way to...

May I take a moment to express my sincere thanks for...

When you find a need to (describe your service), I would appreciate the opportunity to show you all the excellent (name products) we can offer you.

It is gratifying to see someone show dedication to _____, and you've done so very commendably.

You can rest assured that (name your product) will justify your confidence.

Salutations may include: Come by anytime, Look forward to your next visit, Best of Luck, Best personal regards, Cordially, Enthusiastically..., When we have some more _____ come in, I will call you.

People don't care how much you know until they know how much you care. Say thank you!

There's little more we can do to give ourselves a lift than expressing an attitude of gratitude. It results in changed feelings on the part of the giver and ultimately influences the attitudes and feelings of the recipient. If you'd like to take charge of your world and work, begin today to be more appreciative and show it.

The following are *thank-you notes* and letters of appreciation I have recently received:

"Dear Mr. Dennis,
I hope that you will enjoy your purchases from Nordstrom Washington Square.
Please let me know if I can help you or your family with your holiday shopping.
Thank you."

"Dear Larry,
Thank you for making your recent purchase from Portland AudioVideo. I am grateful to you as a customer and friend.
I hope you were pleased by your experience with Portland AudioVideo. I know this business will only be successful if you, and all our customers, are impressed enough to continue shopping with us and recommend Portland to friends.
Your thoughts about how you were treated are very important to me. I can't meet every customer, so the phone calls and letters I receive are the most valuable feedback available about the job we're doing. This request is not for show! It is a genuine plea for your comments on how we can serve you. My phone number is 641-3510 and the address is shown below.
I know your time is valuable, and if you call or write I promise it won't be wasted. I will take action on your comments."
Sincerely,"

"Larry,
It was a pleasure to assist you with your suit and tie selection.
Please call upon me again for your future wardrobe and gift items.
Thanks!"

"Dear Mr. Dennis,

Thanks for stopping by our men's department in Yakima. It is always such a pleasure to see you. I hope that the night-shirt you purchased will work out for you.

I also would like to inform you that the dress shirts you requested in a cotton pinpoint are not available at a sale price. I called all Washington region, Oregon region, and several of our California stores. It seems that no one had a solid cotton on sale. We do have several at regular price, as I'm sure you are aware. I will keep my eyes open for you the night we set up for our next sale, June's half-yearly "Father's Day Sale." Hope to see you soon.

Sincerely,"

There is no doubt that I will return to Nordstrom again and for future clothing and gift needs.

"Dear Larry:

Thank you for thinking of me and sending the article about company names. Last time on the phone I meant to acknowledge you for the nice letter you sent me about my newsletter. It was deeply appreciated also.

You know I respect your opinion and the above means more to me because of it.

Expect the best,"

Saying "Thank you" is one of the simplest and best ways to get repeat business. Not saying it is a sure way to lose repeat business. When you take a moment to show an attitude of gratitude, both you and your customers will profit.

Business will continue to go where invited and remain where appreciated.

What else can you do to up your "niceness" quotient, the degree to which you treat your customers in winning ways?

No More Give Aways

A client recalls: I pulled up to the gas pump, took a deep breath, and asked the attendant to fill 'er up. While the tank guzzled gallon after gallon, I managed to overhear a conversation at the next pump. As another customer paid for her gas, she asked the attendant for a map of the state.

"Are you kidding, lady, nobody around here has given away maps in about five years," he said.

"So where can I get one?" she asked meekly.

"Beats me," the attendant said, as he walked away. "I guess you're gonna have to break down and buy one."

After a few moments, the woman, obviously confused and disappointed, drove off.

Many businesses have tightened their promotional budgets and stopped giving away free gifts. They hope no one will notice. But people have noticed. Social observer and author, Erma Bombeck, recently asked her readers if they remembered those free maps, calendars, key rings and rain bonnets they used to receive.

"Once upon a time," she wrote, "businessmen in the country used to court consumers. They wanted their business, and to remind them of this they would give them presents. Not big ones, but little reminders you could use."

Meanwhile, a customer can't get the windshield washed or the oil checked let alone get a free highway map at many stations today.

That's a good clue to the proper treatment of any customer. Maybe some things are too costly to give away.

But service and politeness are not. **Quality is free."**

Your customers...any businesses' customers...will come back where they are appreciated. We can show our appreciation by smiling and providing quick, extra service. And by saying "Thank you."

Conclusion

Our son Barry returned from running in the Moscow World Peace marathon in 1989. He stayed in the largest hotel in the world—35,000 rooms. It was the only hotel in Moscow. I've asked hundreds of people in my audiences what word they thought Barry heard most often while he was visiting the U.S.S.R. Their responses: "perestroika," "glasnost," "please," "thank you," and so on. Barry said that the word he heard more often than any other was "nyet." When he asked for washcloths the answer was "nyet." Soap: "nyet." Toilet paper: "nyet." Before he got his questions or requests out of his mouth, the answer was normally "nyet"—no.

That negative attitude may have been one of the chief factors on the downfall of the communist political system. There were too many "nos."

If you and I want to run successful businesses that experience repeat customers, we must develop the ability to say "yes." Yesterday I pulled up at the back gate of a mass merchandising company that sells, in addition to other things, lumber. I asked if I could come in the back way and walk through, buy some lumber, and then pick it up at the same place. The man at the back gate said, "Nope, you'll have to go around to the front. Don't park back here."

He didn't say, "I'm sorry" or "I wish you could," he

just said, "Nope." I found his abruptness offensive. Although I went to the front as he asked, I would have done it more willingly and readily and been more likely to be a repeat customer if he had just said, "I'm sorry, they won't let us," or "I'm sorry, we can't let you," or "If you don't mind."

The example we cited in Chapter 3 of someone drawing a million dollars out of the bank because of the bank's refusal to validate a parking voucher is a dramatic example of how important it is to develop the mentality to say "yes." How can you develop your ability to be adept at adapting this "yes" concept to every area of your business?

Use the following six steps to repeat business:
- **Reliability:** Keep promises, implied or implicit.
- **Extra Mile:** Always do more than you are paid for or are expected to do.
- **Pleasing Personality:** Be courteous and sincere.
- **Enthusiasm:** Remain positive, regardless of the situation.
- **Action:** Serve customers immediately .
- **Thank You:** Be appreciative and show it .

Repeat business makes it worthwhile to spend the money we do on advertising and marketing. But that is the smallest portion of the return we get. People who continue to favor us with their purchases are telling us every time they spend a dollar with us that they approve of the way we do things. They are telling us with their patronage that they value the relationship that has been established. We value them for more than the economic benefit they represent. We value them as real people who thrive on our attention, our respect for their opinions, our understanding of their need to be praised for their buying decisions.

And we value them for other reasons: They bring to us validation of the quality of our products and services—which is a reflection of our own excellence. It is worthwhile working hard and thoughtfully to achieve that merit in the eyes of other persons.

Attention Managers!

The Manager's Training Guide to Repeat Business is the tool designed expecially for you to apply the infomation in Larry W. Dennis's book to the employee programs. This training guide provides you with a step-by-step approach to follow in ten weekly customer service team meetings. You will energize your team and create more new and repeat customers for your products or services.

For information call or write Larry W. Dennis at:

Turbo Management Systems™
5440 S.W. Westgate Drive, Suite 340
Portland, Oregon 97221
Telephone: 503-292-1919

Larry W. Dennis, the author of Repeat Business, is available for speaking engagements, seminars and workshops. He teaches the principles of acquiring and keeping Repeat Business in a fresh, compelling way.

The ideas that form the framework of Repeat Business are available to your company on the patented Psycho-Actualized Learning System (PAL). PAL provides the most effective way to create the behaviors necessary to make permanent the application of the dynamic ideas in Repeat Business.

Ask Larry W. Dennis to create a customized customer service video training program for your company.

For more information about speaking engagements, training or the PAL customer video programs, contact:

Turbo Management Systems™

5440 S. W. Westgate Drive, Suite 340
Portland, Oregon 97221
Telephone: 503-292-1919

About the Author

Larry W. Dennis is the energetic founder of Turbo Management Systems. Through his company, Dennis has been responsible for improving the profits of hundreds of businesses whose key managers have learned the important principles of repeat business practices. Dennis is the inventor of the video training system, Psycho-Actualized Learning, the author of three books, and is a dedicated father who has been profiled in "Secrets of Raising Teenagers Successfully." Dennis also serves on the Business Advisory Council of Warner Pacific College.

Please Send Me:

_____ Copies *Empowering Leadership* $14.95 each

_____ Copies *Repeat Business* $11.95 each

_____ Copies *How To Turbo Charge You* $14.95 each

_____ Copies *Communicating For Results* $9.95 each

_____ Copies *Making Moments Matter* $9.95 each

_____ Videos *Remembering Names and More* $69.95 each

_____ Videos *Anyone Can Juggle* $19.95 each

_____ Demo videos of *Turbo Presentations* $19.95 each

_____ Empowering Leadership *Ball Caps* $9.95 each

_____ Please send me complete information about the training services of Turbo Management Systems - No Charge

(Please add $2.00 for shipping and handling for first item and $1.00 for each additional item)

For the total amount of: $_____

Check enclosed for $_____   *or*   *Master Card/Visa* _____

Account Number _____

Expiration Date _____

Name: _____

Address: _____

_____

_____

Phone: _____   *Fax:* _____

Please Mail Or Fax Order To:
Turbo Management Systems
5440 S.W. Westgate Drive
Suite 340
Portland, Oregon 97221
(503) 292-1919
For Fast Response
Fax: (503) 292-2118